SOMETIMES I FEEL LIKE RUNNING AWAY FROM HOME

SOMETIMES I FEEL LIKE RUNNING AWAY FROM HOME

Saving Your Sanity and Refreshing Your Spirit
When You Feel Trapped by Your Own Life

ELIZABETH CODY NEWENHUYSE

BETHANY HOUSE PUBLISHERS
MINNEAPOLIS, MN 55438

Published by Bethany House Publishers
A Division of Bethany Fellowship, Inc.
11300 Hampshire Avenue South
Minneapolis, Minnesota 55438

Printed in the United States of America

Library of Congress Cataloging-in-Publication Data

Newenhuyse, Elizabeth Cody.
  Sometimes I feel like running away from home /
  Elizabeth Newenhuyse.
     p. cm.
    1. Wives—Religious life. 2. Wives—Conduct of life.
  3. Mothers—Religious life. 4. Mothers—Conduct of life.
  5. Women—Psychology. I. Title.
BV4527.N46 1993
248.8'43—dc20   93-8115
ISBN 1-55661-317-2   CIP

Elizabeth Newenhuyse is a writer whose byline has appeared dozens of times in Christian periodicals and on two previous books. Formerly Senior Editor of *Marriage Partnership*, she and her husband and daughter live near Chicago.

Contents

1
The Care and Feeding of Your Soul

HAVE YOU EVER had a three-in-the-morning attack? You know the kind: You unaccountably wake up and start thinking. Gloomy thoughts, like *I have no real friends.* Scary thoughts, like *Where's the money going to come from?* Unsettling thoughts, like *I've lived half my life. What am I going to do with the rest of it?*

Eventually, you roll over and go back to sleep. And in the bustle of morning, those wee-hours thoughts are forgotten. Lately, though, some of my three-a.m. reflections have been sticking with me—especially the one about the rest of my life. And some other things have been happening to me that I can't ignore.

One evening recently my husband fell asleep on the couch. In the early years of our marriage I would attempt to rouse him by hollering "Fritz . . . *Fritz* . . . FRITZ!" thinking that it would be nice for a man and wife to retire at the same time. I don't do that anymore, because nothing short of my screaming "Cubs win the pennant!" or "Killer tidal wave! Run for your life!" will wake him once he's out.

So I went into the bedroom alone, closed the door, and read a book by a pastor. My daughter, who hates going to bed, was mercifully asleep. The dog was denied access. The night was quiet. I often read in bed, but for some reason this felt different. It sure wasn't the book—which was well-meaning, but dull. Maybe it was because I'm so starved for diversion that having the bed against a different wall constitutes a form of entertainment (we'd rearranged the bedroom furniture). I don't know . . . but *everything* in me relaxed. I felt my entire nervous system uncoil . . . I felt at peace . . . on top of the world . . . Maybe tomorrow I'd even balance my checkbook . . .

Then I thought, *This really is pathetic.* Twenty minutes of solitary reading—and a boring book, at that—and it's as if I'd escaped to Club Med. I must be pretty desperate for time to myself. Or maybe it was that I needed time *with* myself.

Just an ordinary spring evening . . . but it made me think. Am I such a prisoner of the mundane; are the streams of life inside me *this* drained?

Soon after that incredible incident I started having a recurring dream: I am cleaning house. A sense of obligation permeates even my subconscious. As I clean, I come across a cage with a bird in it—a canary or parakeet. The bird is fluttering at the bottom of the cage, barely alive, because I have forgotten to feed it. I have forgotten to feed it because I've forgotten I even own the poor thing. Over and over, I awake, feeling anxious, guilty . . . and a little sad.

The bird, I believe, represents my spirit, and the mental and emotional parts of me that I have "starved" through neglect. Starved because of the guilt that tells me I have no right to plaintively ask, *What about my own created soul?* Starved because I haven't, until recently, taken the time to step back and get some perspective on what God really wants.

The dream was not my only warning light. The most overwhelming signal was the loss of my beloved father in 1991. When you stare into the hole left by that kind of loss, your own finitude stares back at you. I told myself: I have only so much energy to go around. Am I really doing what I want to do? What about the next forty years? Sure, I'm busy, but am I pouring my life . . . my self . . . into things that will not last and don't really matter in the long run?

MAKE AN "I-WANT LIST"

Does that sound like a childish, selfish statement to you? It shouldn't. We all have deep dreams, desires, wishes, hopes. It may help to articulate—even write down—a few of those dreams (and what's keeping you from achieving them.) Take a few minutes now and make a short, specific list. Then think about how you could turn your "I-wants" into "I-haves."

Here are a few examples to get you started:

- I want a friend who builds me up.
- I want to take a weekend just to be by myself.
- I want to change churches.
- I want to write children's books.
- I want more fun and diversity in my life.
- I want to get to know my sister better.
- I want to spend more time enjoying nature.
- I want to get more sleep.

It's easy for most of us women to overlook our own needs in the press of life's demands. It's easy to put our own soul on hold while we're giving to everyone else. *Jesus first, others second, yourself last*—didn't we learn something like that in Sunday school? We scatter ourselves like bread crumbs, and whole flocks of hungry birds consume us.

Then we feel guilty when we wish our families would

leave us alone for once!—like the newlywed I know, who was relishing an evening to herself. She called it "my sacred four hours" when her husband was away at a class. It was so precious to her that she felt resentful, interrupted, when her husband returned home early!

Guilty and wistful, we wonder what it would be like to return to a hobby we once enjoyed. Maybe we'd like to take a day of silent retreat somewhere to gain a sense of recollecting all that feels scattered and lost in our lives. But we can't justify the time off. (In another of my recurring dreams, I am catching a plane for a vacation by myself to a warm climate, in a nice hotel . . .) We know we're scattering our energies all over the place, doing too much, responsible for too much. Like a home video, we come in and out of focus as to what's really important. Did we ever even *know* what's important?

How uneasily we sense the slipping away of the hours . . . months . . . years. But we don't know how to grab onto those segments of time and make them count. "Why do you spend your life and your energies on things that do not satisfy?" the Lord asks us through Isaiah. Now, there's a good question.

Time alone to renew. Kindness to yourself in order to rebuild. Investing yourself on what really matters. Sounds wonderful, but who has the time? It's all that most of us can to do chase after our children, pay the bills, go to work, attack the clutter piles.

Let's face it. Any focus on "me" seems entirely inappropriate for the Christian woman. I used to work as a magazine editor, and we got a lot of periodicals in the office including various women's magazines, the general-circulation kind that glut the supermarket check-out lines. I was always aghast at their intense focus on self—finding the perfect eye shadow, doing the latest workout, climbing the career ladder. I thought, *Here we live in a dying world—with violence in our schools—and I'm supposed to worry about using the right olive oil?* Christians tend to think this way.

Dear friend, pay attention: We as Christian women, daughters of the Most High King, have better reasons than anyone else to care for ourselves. *Without guilt.* We make commitments to church, home, work; take seriously the care of our husbands and children; expend our energies on umpteen worthy activities in the community. Why is it so hard to spend some time on ourselves? Inside *and* out.

I try to approach every significant aspect of my life with the question: How do I do this in a *Christian* manner? How can I be a better mom, a better wife, a better friend? How can I radiant Christ to others through my work, through my service at church, through hospitality in my home? All good intentions—but sometimes they diminish me. They wear me out!

We need to give ourselves permission to *recharge* occasionally; to figure out what to give up and what to hold on to; to learn how to be our own true selves, regardless of the expectations of others; to be at peace with the way God created us as individuals.

Through this volume you hold in your hands, I want you to learn to allow yourself some kindness, some inner refreshment. I want to offer you some mini-vacations, stress-relievers, wisdom from insightful people.

I hope to give you some practical pointers: How do you achieve healthy relationships? How do you break the habit of downgrading yourself? How do you allow others to help you? How do you achieve your dreams? How do you find time with God?

Self is not a "four-letter word." Too often we take the burned bacon, eat the heel of the bread, give up our TV show for someone else's preference in the family. Our morning shower doubles as prayer time, strategy time . . . as long as no one interrupts.

It's hard to admit that we really don't want to help out in the church nursery or bring a three-bean salad to the potluck—maybe we don't even want to *go* to the potluck. We would rather relax at home. But isn't saying 'no' unchristian somehow? Doesn't it sound like we are uncommitted? Even if we're dead-tired after work, we grimly set our face to making dinner. It's what a good wife and mother should do, isn't it?

We run ourselves ragged. We give out and give out and give out—scattering grain from our meager stores—while the starving bird that is our spirit weakly flutters, hoping for a bit of grain for herself. We're tired and we don't know why. We listen patiently to everyone else's problems; we work hard to satisfy the needs of our family; all the while tuning out the still small voice that asks, "Where is the house you will build for Me?"

"Okay, I struggle with all that," you say. "But *how* do I make the changes?"

Through some very difficult experiences, I've begun to discover ways to refocus my life—how to recharge, and to live at rest.

At the time my father got sick I was still working full time. Being editor of a magazine may sound glamorous, but it is very mentally draining. The job requires that you show up at the office even if you're having a bad-hair day, your child is in the school play and you have to make his costume, and your checkbook badly needs to be balanced.

My first book had just come out and I had been asked to write another. I was ecstatic. The host of a nationally broadcast Christian radio program called and said he thought my book was good. Could I drive down to the studio and be interviewed live? Was he kidding? Of course I could!

But as I sat there in the studio trying to be witty and articulate, I felt a big gap inside. I kept picturing Dad at home . . . in bed . . . listening to the radio. Mom was on the other bed. Dad couldn't stand up very well because he had a cyst in his brain that affected his balance. He needed surgery.

It was weird: Just as one of the most important people in my life was slipping away from me, a super big dream was coming true for me at the same time.

IN THE GARDEN

"When Mary found this garden it looked quite dead," Colin proceeded. "Then something began pushing things up out of the soil and making things out of nothing. One day things weren't there and another they were. I had never watched things before, and it made me feel very curious. I kept saying to myself: 'What is it? What is it?' It's something. It can't be nothing! I don't know its name, so I call it Magic. I have never seen the sun rise, but Mary and Dickon have, and from what they tell me I am sure that is Magic, too. Something pushes it up and draws it. Sometimes since I've been in the garden, I've looked up through the trees at the sky and I have a strange feeling of being happy, as if something were pushing and drawing in my chest and making me breathe fast. Magic is always pushing and drawing and making things out of nothing. Everything is made out of Magic, leaves and trees, flowers and birds, badgers and foxes, and squirrels and people. So it must be all round us. In this garden—in all the places."
— Frances Hodgson Burnett

Christians know what the Magic is—the transforming power of God's healing love, which can "make things out of nothing," whether it is an abandoned patch of weeds transformed into a beautiful garden, or an invalid boy, like Colin in Burnett's story, made well and reunited with his father.

Mary Lennox was led by a robin to the key that unlocked The Secret Garden. What would be the key that would open the door to your own "magic garden," your place or re-creation and renewal?

After Dad's surgery, complications set in. For weeks we made the thirty-five-mile trip to Chicago to visit him in the hospital. He was on a respirator and couldn't speak. He just looked at me and held my hand. He liked me to sponge his face and hands. He probably needed the human contact more than the cool dampness on his skin. I'd sit and watch him after he'd fallen asleep.

And then one day he was gone.

Everything changed after Dad died. Including me. Several weeks later I had lunch with a friend who had lost both parents by the time she was thirty. My emotions were lurching all over the place as I shared my grief, one thought tumbling over another. My good friend said to me, "You have to be kind to yourself now. You're more fragile than you know."

I paused to reflect. Her words opened something in my grieving soul, the way the increase in light opens leaves in April. She gave me permission to think about myself, to care about myself, to take responsibility for being good to myself in a way I hadn't before. To consider myself important and sometimes needy. To ask, as Dad so often did, "How *are* you?" and to mean it.

I began to see how important it was to take notice of my own needs, to intentionally take a day off now and then, to stop beating myself. To come to terms with who I am—strengths and limitations alike.

I began to take a hard look at my life: How do I *not* squander it? How can I be kind to myself? What are my real priorities? How do I give myself more space, more rest, more peace? *What does the Lord require?*

You may not have a friend who has given you the same permission. Well, take it from me—ask yourself some of the same questions I did, and stumble onto some of your own insights. You may find that you are clamped in the jaws of over-responsibility and can't figure out how to be free of it—without feeling guilty. A lot of women are feeling exactly as you do.

Said simply, I hope to place your hand in the palm of God again—our God who is life and mercy and strength itself. Our God is merciful. His compassion for you flows without failing. Gently He's been leading me—laboring *Pilgrim's Progress*-like under my baggage of over-busy bad habits—toward a surer sense of what it means to belong to Him. He is teaching me how to apply new life-giving insights to my life as a woman, wife, mother, and friend.

Do you know your life's focus? Have you taken God's offer of guilt-free living into your heart? Or are you still anxiously groping for meaning, importance, a reason to go on? Maybe you're just plain tired out.

These pages are offered in the hope that you will be helped to know yourself a little better, to take time for and with yourself, to live deeply, richly, more fully in Christ. We may even have a good time!

As my friend offered her gift of kindness to me, this book is my offering of friendship to you. Find a front-porch swing, or an armchair by the fire. Pour yourself some lemonade, or make some hot cocoa. Turn on the answering machine, and tune out the demands of the world for a while.

We've got things to talk about.

2

A Bad Case of the I Shoulds

ONE OF THE GROUND-BREAKING FILMS of our generation was *Kramer vs. Kramer*. In it, Dustin Hoffman played the sympathetic, caring dad fighting for custody of his young son—against his wife, played by Meryl Streep, who had callously left the family to "find herself."

For me, the most heart-tugging scene in the film comes when Meryl Streep stands motionless across the street from where her son plays—wearing her business-like trench coat—just watching him.

The message conveyed in the film was this: No good mother leaves her children; and certainly not to find herself.

To abandon her children goes against the deepest instincts of a woman. Anyone who puts her needs before those of her dependent preschooler seems unnatural, almost monstrous.

Most of us are not Mrs. Kramers, but who hasn't felt the urge to bolt and run away from home at times? And who among us has not felt selfish or guilty about going out for an evening with the girls, for example, instead of staying at home with our families? We leave dinner in the oven and a list of instructions. Heaven forbid our husbands or children must fend for themselves for three of four hours!

More of us are brow-beaten by the image of the *godly mother* than the individualistic mother. We imagine Suzannah Wesley raising her throng of children to do great and mighty things for the Lord, never leaving dinner bubbling in the kettle while she went out into the community. Or, you can bring it into this century: Reading interviews of magazine editors with well-known Christian women, we get the idea that most of them *invariably* give their families first priority. Surely these women *never* long for more freedom. They never feel guilty or crabby; they never get sick or have doubts; they never have ragged fingernails . . . Life in Christian media-land is so serene.

But in the glossy world of the media, every problem has a solution. Every celebrity has a supportive spouse, contented children, and a disciplined devotional life. No wonder the rest of us feel like . . . well, you know how you feel. We generally come down with a bad case of the *I shoulds*.

What is it that makes *you* feel guilty and inadequate? We all have our guilt-ridden dramas-in-real-life to recount. Some days my dramas feel more like epic sagas. Here's a sampling:

Guilt-drama #1: One day I was at my computer trying to write. The words were not coming very well, so I decided to take our dog for a long tramp. He needed the exercise and so did I.

I'd gotten only a couple of blocks away from our house, and I was concentrating on solving some writing problems—when *pit-pat, pit-pat,* came the sound of little feet. My little daughter had followed me.

"Mom needs to be by herself for a while," I explained to Amanda. "Anyway, weren't you playing with Megan?"

Her eager, shining little face showed disappointment. In her world Mom was always available. Don't get me wrong, I believe availability is a good thing. "I wanted to be with you," she said. "Don't you want to be with me?"

A great cloud of witnesses—Suzannah Wesley, Edith Schaeffer, Elisabeth Elliot, Beverly LaHaye—rose up in my mind and said as one: *What kind of mother are you?*

OH, NO, NOT HER AGAIN!

For Christians, the Proverbs 31 woman represents a shining ideal. But she can be a roadblock to growth, because we know we can never be that wonderful. We may even view ourselves as the Proverbs 32 woman ("She considers a bed and sleeps in it").

The problem is, Christians often take good ideas and make them into legalisms: Always get up early; do not be idle; work vigorously at home and out of the home; help the poor. Then, if we fail to meet these and other requirements for perfection, we feel we have failed in God's eyes.

We simply cannot take the Proverbs 31 woman as a literal example to follow. (Not if she rises before dawn and her lamp does not go out at night.) If you take the verses in the context of Proverbs as a whole, you will see that the portrait represents a catalogue of the virtues highlighted throughout the book: diligence, wisdom, fear of the Lord. All important things to strive for. But don't castigate yourself because your life doesn't look like the Proverbs 31 ideal.

"Of course, honey," I caved in. "Come along." I am not some self-involved feminist type like the Kramer character. I am a Bible-believing Christian woman who quit her job so she could work at home and spend more time with her child. I would go for a much-needed walk alone another time. I did enjoy the walk, of course. Amanda, at eight, is a delightful companion. But all the way I was dragging along the ball-and-chain of guilt. By my own choice, the walk never led me to the place of refreshment I so needed.

Guilt-drama #2: The other night I got a phone call from a woman at church. "Someone told me that you were interested in teaching Sunday school next year," she began.

"Um, gee, sure . . . I don't know," I said. (Forceful. Decisive. Taking control of my own life.)

"Oh . . . maybe I heard wrong," she said. There was almost a catch in her voice.

I envisioned her going through the church directory in a hopeless, quixotic quest for teachers. By now she had reached the N's and had probably signed up about two volunteers, all for the preschool classes. I sighed. The *I-should* virus was really starting to ravage my defenses. "Well, if you find you need . . ."

She jumped at the opening. "Can I sign you up as a substitute, then?"

"Okay. Sure."

No doubt I'll get a call about eight o'clock some sub-zero Sunday morning in January, asking if I can pinch-hit with the junior high—a roomful of boys with breaking voices and too much energy and too many hormones. In a mid-sized church like ours, after all, everyone has to pitch in. (Pointing finger: This means *you!*)

Guilt-drama #3: As I was writing this morning, I went into the kitchen. (Never mind why.) As I did so I tripped over the doorway. (Don't ask me how.) And I slammed my elbow into the door frame—right on that bone that sends shooting pain all the way up your arm. It swelled immediately and hurt like crazy. *I should rest and elevate it,* I thought. *Maybe put some ice on it.* Then, *I will. In awhile. But first there's work I should do.*

Why do I do this to myself? Why do I allow the *I shoulds* to run my life? Why do you?

We may even feel quite fulfilled in our lives—we're active, busy doing good things, raising our kids, loving our husbands, serving the church, maybe even holding down a job outside the home. But what we don't realize is that while we do these things, we're short-changing ourselves, denying our souls and our bodies the rest, the quiet, the refreshment they so desperately need. Then something happens and we realize we have an empty longing.

It's wonderful to be a Christian woman today. But a misinterpretation of what it means to live that out can wear us down. We hear about misspent youth—what about misspent womanhood?

Traditionally, women have been the backbone of the church. We all grew up knowing energetic, dedicated women—the ones who taught generations of Sunday school students the hand motions to "This Little Light of Mine," the ones who always washed the kitchen towels, polished the altar, collated the newsletter, the women who out-lasted one pastor after another. Though many of us may not have the time anymore to imitate this model, we feel like we *should* imitate her. We feel we *ought* to pray more, *ought* to read the Bible more, *ought* to gather canned goods for the needy, and *ought* to teach Sunday school.

For most of us there's the phenomenon of being "on-call." If you are a mother you never entirely check out, even in your sleep. After all, who hears the child cry out in the night, even through two closed doors? Some husbands pitch in willingly around the house, and that's great, but there's a sense that the ultimate responsibility for the children's well-being, the well-being of your marriage, your aging parents, and your friends rests on you.

The *I shoulds* sap our energy, keeping us from concentrating on what really matters to God and to us. They distort our vision of ourselves and others. And like a virus that can lie dormant in your system all your life, they're very, very hard to shake.

Permaguilt

A friend of mine has coined the term "permaguilt" to identify the feeling that never goes away. Like the permafrost that lies a few feet under the Arctic tundra, winter and summer, permaguilt is always there just beneath the surface—that vague sense that no matter how well we're managing our lives, there's something we should, or should not, be doing.

To get a better handle on this issue, it might be helpful to distinguish between "being-guilt" and "doing-guilt." Yes, friends, the great river of guilt has tributaries. "Being-guilt" is guilt over who you are, or who you feel you should be. "Doing-guilt" is guilt over what you're doing or not doing, how you're using your time.

Have you ever thought:
- I should be thin.
- I should have more friends.
- I should get a job.
- I shouldn't be working outside the home.
- I should keep the house cleaner.
- I shouldn't be so meticulous.
- I should be a better mom.
- I should have a hobby.
- I shouldn't spend so much time on my hobby.
- I should manage my time better.
- I should pray more.

And the list goes on. I'm sure you could probably add to it.

I've struggled with many of these shoulds and should-nots for years. For the longest time I tried to battle the shoulds by sheer force of will—or by trying to copy someone else. Take for example time management and organization. I made a once-and-for-all resolution at the beginning of the year that I would buy a Day-Timer, keep a comprehensive calendar, make lists and adhere to them, never waste a moment. No more forgetting a birthday; no more spending hours searching for some critical paperwork because I didn't have a system in place for organizing it.

I used to admire a woman I worked with who brought

a Day-Timer to every meeting. When she said, "I'll just check my calendar," I admired her and wanted to be more like her.

So, I ordered a Day-Timer. It came in the mail. You know the kind—a leather-bound pocket calendar with spiral-bound inserts for each month. Pages for listing things to do today, and things to be done by a certain date. Expense records. People to contact. When you finish a month, you file the notebook away in a nice permanent file box.

Well, the whole thing is filed away in that box, and sits on the bottom shelf of my bookcase! It was all wrong for me. I have large, scrawly handwriting. The pocket format was just too small. And I am not a salesman with dozens of appointments and the need for careful expense records, anyway. My life is just not that structured. The wall calendar I got free from the company and the small pads of paper for making to-do lists work just fine—for me.

In reality, when I purchased the Day-Timer I was buying an image I hoped to live up to—that of the organized, professional working woman with just the right accessories. But I discovered that just as I am not a business-jacket person, I am not a pocket-calendar person. If I hadn't been given a beautiful leather briefcase when I left my magazine editor's job, I would still be carrying my canvas tote around. I think Day-Timers are fine quality products. If they work for you, great. They didn't work for me.

Maybe you have succumbed to the temptation to try to be something or someone you are not. I was trying to emulate someone else, trying to live up to the expectations of others. Or rather, what I thought others expected of me. I guess that's why they call this kind of thinking complex. I suffered from *being-guilt*.

It still hits me sometimes—the feeling that I am inadequate, that I should be somehow better than I am. But now I recognize it for what it is, and I try not to let it drive me.

Set Your Hearts . . .

If you're weighed down by wanting to be like someone else—if you're letting other people's demands and expectations run your life, you need to adjust your focus.

"Seek *first* the kingdom of God," Jesus says. That's not just a command, but a wonderful bit of wisdom for life.

The lesson God has been patiently teaching me is this: If I would truly live in Him, serve Him, glorify Him, I have to put Him first. I have to stop scattering myself around because of guilt, and focus on Him. As you and I learn to live within this framework, everything else will fall into place.

"Being-guilt," at its core, is a profoundly spiritual issue. It keeps us from remembering that "We are God's workmanship, created in Christ Jesus to do good works . . ." (Ephesians 2:10). (Those good works may or may not include teaching Sunday school.) We must never lose sight of the fact that first and foremost we are to be growing in the image of Jesus Christ, whose life on earth was our model of unhurried trust in God. He showed us the perfect way— to listen quietly for God's voice, and then to obey Him. We cannot live this way if we are given daily to a nervous, frenzied pace.

If we are God's workmanship, created in Christ Jesus, should we care for ourselves any less than He cares for us? In Chapter 9, we'll look at how to give God more time, more quality time. (And for many Christian women, finding time for God is guilt-inducing issue Numero Uno.)

For now, I would like to suggest you look through the Scriptures, using a good study Bible, one with a useful concordance. Find passages that focus on pleasing God not men; on setting your mind on things above; on belonging to Christ.

Underline them; commit them to memory; put them up in your kitchen or office on Post-it notes. Then determine that no matter what you do, or what path in life you choose, you will learn to rest in His approval over and above the approval and demands of others.

A woman's gift, and often her burden, is the ability to juggle. But it's easy for many of us to run from one thing to the next, doing a lot of different things *semi-well*. It seems we would do better selecting certain priorities for our lives. This would include caring for the people He has entrusted to us, and exercising the gifts He has given us. Maybe our motto should be: *Do fewer things, but do them well*.

"Being-guilt" is not only a spiritual issue, but a relational issue. We women tend to judge our lives against the lives of others. We compare and contrast, envy and covet. We feel guilty if we don't measure up . . . we feel more guilty because we know we shouldn't compare.

Listen to Paul's reminder to the Galatians: "Each one should test his own actions. Then he can take pride in himself, without comparing himself to somebody else" (6:4). Whether it's a woman using a Day-Timer, a glamorous media image, a friend who is thinner than you are, or one who seems more spiritually mature, we must stop judging ourselves and comparing ourselves to others. Have you ever thought that someone might envy *you*? A new concept.

Face it. There will *always* be someone who is more successful than you are, more beautiful, more spiritual, more together. You and I can waste a lot of energy comparing ourselves to others and feeling depressed when we come out on the short end. God wants us to judge ourselves against His standards. Then be the best you can be with what He has given you. Comparisons only devalue the unique person that God made you, and the unique person that He made someone else.

It's time to declare war on all that would destroy our inner peace, those poisonous agents of discontent. Are you weary of being restless and dissatisfied? Do you feel like you're climbing a mountain whose summit recedes farther and farther just when you think you've reached the top?

Today we live in the updrafts of what has been coined

"upward-mobility." We are constantly bombarded with the seeming success of others. We can't turn on the TV without looking in on the lifestyles of the rich and famous. Most sitcoms do not portray life as it really is. Maybe you've already guessed that. Is it a plot to make me dissatisfied with my life and to want someone else's? Real godly contentment, according to the Scriptures, is downright countercultural.

So what do we do? For starters, we could stop watching so much TV. We could throw out those glitzy mail-order catalogs that offer things we are not going to buy anyway. (I don't know about you, but every time I flip through one of those things, my house starts to feel like "Dogpatch, U.S.A.") The subtle message in these catalogs, women's magazines, and TV is that these things—whether it be houses, cars, furniture, clothes, vacations to exotic places— are more important than anything. They are more necessary and more valuable than you or your family. Well, they aren't. If anything, it's part of a gargantuan lie that is more dangerous than, or at least as dangerous as, some other media hype that Christians get upset about. All of this stuff appeals to our latent materialism.

Another way to deal with our tendency to compare ourselves to others and feel inadequate is to open up with other women about this issue. Are there certain friends you secretly envy or compare yourself to? Tell them so—but do it gently and with humor. You may both have a good laugh over it. Get to know people who seem to have learned the secret of contentment. I have a few friends who really don't care or worry about what the other guy has or does. They're a priceless influence on me.

Third, ask yourself whether envy or comparison is really a negative for you. Maybe it isn't. You may admire someone else's clothes, for example, but also know that that woman spends far more time and money shopping than you would ever care to. On the other hand, we all need *positive* models. There is such a thing as healthy comparison. For example, if there's a woman in your church who has weathered personal tragedy with serenity and spiritual maturity, sit at her feet. Learn from her.

Fourth, remember that envy, like so many other things, can be a knee-jerk habit we fall into, automatically comparing someone else's house to ours, feeling diminished by a friend's success, whatever. When you catch yourself in the act, stop right there. Take a deep breath, and think, *No! I will not get caught in this trap again!* Do that enough and maybe you'll get out of the habit. (Don't console yourself by comparing downward either: "At least we're better off than the Smiths. He lost his job and she had to go to work. . . .")

Fifth, envy is sinful because it wastes your precious life. Just that. It's wrong. Whatever the world says, God's Word teaches us not to covet, not to lust, not to take pride in the things of this world, which pass away. Maybe you and your husband have chosen to live at a more modest level than your neighbors. Stand firm in that choice. Seek out like-minded individuals. Be content in knowing that God honors your decision.

It's My Party, and I'll Live for God if I Want To!

Finally, we have to consider what God is calling us to do with our own life—not what others are telling us we "should" do with it. John says, "The world and its desires pass away, but the man who does the will of God lives forever" (1 John 2:17). We need to listen hard to our own inner convictions and not try to live out someone else's agenda.

God gives us clues as to what He wants for us. For example, do you find yourself drawn to certain people and pursuits over and over? That's a clue. For some reason we tend to think that what gives us peace and fulfillment— what feels "right"—must not be what God wants, as if God's design for our lives is difficult to decipher and harder to achieve!

I know a woman who, in her late thirties, is finally responding to what she feels is God's call to her to minister to others through a career in contemporary Christian music. She said, "For the longest time I felt that this wasn't what God wanted for me." But whenever she had free time she dove for the piano like a baseball player sliding into home base. When she sang in church, people were profoundly moved by the power of her songs.

HAPPY RETIREMENT TO ME!

Maybe you've attended a retirement or testimonial dinner for someone where all the guests stood up and said glowing things about the honoree. If someone gave a retirement dinner for you, what would you want them to say? Your spouse? Your friends? Your colleagues? Your pastor? Your children? What do you think they would say?

Of course, discovering that God wants to use your gift doesn't mean everything is suddenly roses. Far from it! For my friend, hours of practicing, making a recording, dealing with music professionals, booking concerts, has added a whole new dimension of pressures and complications to her life. To top it off, as I write this, she is awaiting the birth of her second child—seventeen years after the first! But she and her husband are trusting that God will make a path through the sea of their complicated and challenging lives. And she has the peace that comes from knowing that she has stopped running away from her gift.

On the other hand, *lack* of peace can be a great indicator that we need to make a change, regardless of what society expects. You may be one of the women who has opted for part-time or at-home work in order to spend more time with your family. So am I, and our ranks are growing.

It was partly a lack of peace that nudged me out of my magazine editor's job—lack of peace about my child, lack of peace about what I was doing with my life, lack of peace about who I was. I'm not really the glamorous-working-woman type. Maybe some can fill that role, but not me. It's the Day-Timer thing. I wanted to be home, badly. I believe young children need a mother on hand most of the time . . . a mother who can help give them a childhood. Never mind that I was in "Christian work"—I was still gone too much.

So here I am, at home, at my computer, writing, at peace . . . most of the time. That isn't to say, though, that all my problems are solved—especially the financial ones. But sometimes, when God pulls you beyond the *I shoulds* stage, it means a certain amount of risk. It calls for courage and trust and the willingness to live with uncertainty. I may be sitting comfortably at home, laughing smugly at the commuters who are trying to make their way home through the snow, but I'm still on a challenging path.

Please understand: I'm not saying that every working mom should quit her job, or that every at-home mom should go into business for herself. Despite what some experts may say, there is no one rule for everyone. There may be a time when I decide to go back to full-time employment. Each of us has to make these decisions based on how we feel God is leading us at the time, not on what friends, society, or the media tell us.

When we stop feeling we have to apologize for every move we make, we will have taken a giant step away from the guilt trap of doing for others and never doing for ourselves. Remembering who you are as a child of God is the first step toward freedom and toward doing God's will for *you.*

The other kind of guilt I mentioned was "doing-guilt." It has to do with the fact that I should have cleaned house today. To tell the truth, I ought to have cleaned yesterday. Now it's getting toward dinnertime and the house is looking a little like a landfill. Do you ever feel like whatever you are doing at a given moment is keeping you from doing something else that needs doing? Do you have a "to-do" list with nothing crossed out? You are not alone.

We will get to this debilitating guilt in the next chapter. Meanwhile, I have to start dinner. Maybe there are some fish sticks in the freezer.

3
Attack of the Killer To-Do List

THIS MORNING I TOOK a moment to relax and read the comics in the newspaper. *Sylvia*, that voice of frustrated womanhood, featured this acidic entry "from the journal of the woman who never wastes a moment of her day: This morning, while stopped at the traffic light, I did some embroidery using the pre-threaded needle I keep on the passenger seat; dashed off a note to a shut-in on the stationery I keep above the visor; and partially filled out some medical insurance claim forms."

Don't you hate people like that?

Then there's real live Marian. I was talking to her on the phone some time ago. I have forgotten now what we were discussing, but there's a good possibility we were talking about our mutual guilt. "You know," Marian admitted, "sometimes I worry that, deep down, I'm basically lazy."

I confessed that I wondered the same thing about myself. It was nine-thirty in the morning, after all, and I was still in my robe. (And it was not a Saturday.) How far does this being kind to yourself go, anyway?

I bear little resemblance to *Sylvia's* type-A woman who never wastes a moment. I take my daughter to swimming

33

lessons. All around me I see women reading important-looking books, sorting coupons, and making calligraphy greeting cards while waiting for their kids. I wouldn't be

ARE YOU FIGHTING NATURE?

Like the land, human bio-rhythms have peaks and valleys—times when we're energetic, times when we're sluggish, times when we're creative. We would all do well to recognize these times and try to work within them so we're not fighting against ourselves. I've learned that my "performance chart" looks something like this:

- Up first thing in the morning, especially for creative work
- Steady throughout the morning
- Takes a dive after lunch (naptime!)
- Peaks late in the afternoon
- Crashes to the ground late at night

Naturally, I've learned this the hard way. I know that when I try to work late at night it usually won't be my best effort. On the other hand, by then I'm ready for quiet Bible reading (I'm too restless early in the morning).

This may also apply to a week. I have a hard time getting going on Mondays; it's tough to return to the routine after a Sunday full of church activities, so I try not to overload Monday's calendar. (I said "try!")

Observe over several weeks when you flag and when you fly. Figure out, too, your real sleep needs. (Anything less than seven hours and I'm no good to anyone.) If possible, plan your schedule accordingly, at least the part that you can control. Don't be bound by conventional ideas—I've heard of night owls who go to bed around midnight, sleep for a couple of hours, get up and are productive for another couple of hours, then go back to bed!

surprised if one of them was composing a symphony while doing Kegel exercises.

Actually, I'm probably just jealous. I sit and watch my daughter swimming, and try not to think about the fact that she has just paddled over to the two-fathom deep end. Come to think of it, once I filed my nails during the lesson and felt very virtuous.

Are you ever plagued with "doing-guilt?" Do you live with the sense that you're doing too much, committing yourself to too much? Maybe you feel you're not doing *enough*, or you're doing the right things at the wrong time. Some women are driven to over-do because of a nagging guilt. Their to-do lists are as detailed as the NBA rule book. Others worry about what they *should* be doing, but don't have the time or energy for.

Even as I write, there are a dozen things I *should* be doing. I should buy a baby shower gift; I should be shopping for new shoes for my daughter; I should be paying the Sears bill (it's overdue). The yard needs weeding . . . So what else is new? We have had a lot of rain, though, so I have a good excuse for not getting out there. . . .

I'm beginning to think that I'm not what you'd call compulsive. But I'm not lazy, either . . . Just *relaxed*.

Trend-Setting

I know being relaxed sounds unfashionable. Today's woman is supposed to be driven, occupied, consumed, a perfectionist. But wait a minute, from what I've observed an increasing number of women (and men) are beginning to question the "busyness" that was so trendy in the 80s. They're looking at the price they've paid for being so driven. (In fact, some recent polls indicate that many would trade money for more time off.) So I entertain myself with the thought that, as I read the comics and talk on the phone in my robe, I may be on the cutting edge!

Still, some things *do* have to get done. Whether you're

an at-home working mother or a woman working outside your home, you've probably struggled with this. When I worked full time I made myself crazy trying to fit everything in that had to be done in the limited time I had to do it. When I was home with a baby, I despaired of ever finding time for anything except trying to keep Amanda changed and fed, napped, and protected from injuring herself.

"Doing-guilt" seems to be endemic to the female of the species. Probably because as the old proverb goes, "A woman's work is never done." There is always more to accomplish in a day than there are hours. So those who handle the load successfully must have grabbed hold of a secret that keeps chronic tension and frustration at bay.

THE NAME OF THE GAME IS PITCHING

Sometimes the best thing we can do for ourselves is to complete a task. The principle of "small victories" applies here. Take on something that you know you can finish in fifteen or twenty minutes. Something that involves throwing things away is good. Clean out your magazine basket. Organize one kitchen drawer, preferably the one that gets filled with junk. Pitch those old papers gathering dust in your office.

Now sit back and bask in the feeling that you are on top of things!

The most contented women I know are those who set out to accomplish *what they think is important* in a given day. They have taken the time to evaluate what absolutely has to be done today, and they don't worry about what is left over. There is always tomorrow.

A conversation I had with a woman I'll call Mona

started me thinking about this. We were talking about those women whose houses always look pristine, who seem to know how to add those elegant little touches that make such a difference, like window boxes spilling over with flowers, and handcrafted wreaths on their doors. "Don't you wonder where they find the time?" I sulked.

"I think those women are just more task-oriented, more structured than I'm willing to be," she said. "It's all in how you work. They have their style, and I have mine."

Mona's style *is* more relaxed, and she doesn't apologize for it. She cleans once a week, sometimes watches television in the evenings, plays the piano for relaxation, and occasionally takes the train to downtown Chicago "when my life starts to close in around me."

I used to live across the street from a woman who was an architect. She had an artist's eye for landscaping. Consequently, her yard was a showpiece of curving flagstone paths, carefully varied shrubbery, colorful border plantings. Pam wasn't necessarily guilt-driven or compulsive. It was what she enjoyed, what she knew how to do, and it came easy for her. I was the guilt-driven one—because horticultural efforts like laying a flagstone path bordered with flowers made me want to lie down until the feeling went away.

Marian, who calls herself lazy, could learn from Mona and Pam. She has three boys, kindergarten-age and younger, and has to bear the weight of a home business that requires disciplined attention to deadlines. Marian leaves the dishes, sometimes for days on end. My advice to Marian is that she should lighten up and accept the fact that she hates doing dishes. Maybe she should buy a dishwasher. But she is not lazy.

I whine a lot about not getting stuff done. But I am learning that if I prioritize the use my time, figure out what's important to me, I feel mostly in control of that time, and "doing-guilt" doesn't eat away at my soul.

It's important to me to have a *relatively* clean, uncluttered house. I know people who say, "Ignore the mess," but I can't. I have to spend at least an hour on the house every day. If I didn't, I'd be miserable. It's just that important to me.

I have a friend who likes to look for kids' clothes and toys at garage sales. To Diane, it is a constructive use of her time. I know I'll not find her home on Friday mornings between April and October, because she's out looking for *Nike* shoes that someone's kid outgrew while they were still in great shape.

The first thing is to decide what is important to you and do it, *without* guilt. Likewise, we need to be able to say, "I really don't want to do [such and such]. It is not important to me, and I refuse to feel guilty about it."

How to Begin

If what you're getting done—or not getting done—is an important issue for you, try this: Sit down and make two lists. (Or stand up and burn off a few more calories.) One list should include everything you simply must do in a given week. The other list should include everything you'd like to do on a regular basis, or would like to do if you had the time. Figure out roughly how much time each job or activity takes. *Be sure to allow for "out-of-control" time—a major stressor.* You know what I mean—unexpected interruptions, demands of children, husbands, or employers, the telephone, things that break down, illness. . . . Who hasn't had a week when everything seems to fall apart, and your whole schedule goes down the tubes. There's always next week.

But let's be optimistic! Once you've figured out a schedule that takes into account all your must-dos, like-to-dos, might-get-to-dos, in a given week, you are on your way. If you're feeling industrious, keep a time log each day. Write down everything you actually do, and the time it takes, just for a couple of days. It's revealing to see how we actually use our time, as opposed to how we *think* we're using it.

Then compare the lists. Did you do anything you enjoyed? Are there certain things that are taking up too much time? How many hours do you spend meeting others' demands? How much time does the telephone devour? The TV? What proportion of your time really is out of your control? What could you do about that?

Remember, there's no one "right" way to manage your time. You may be the kind of person who, temperamentally, is more comfortable doing fewer things for longer periods. Don't fall into the trap of thinking you've wasted a day if you haven't accomplished twelve different things.

Keeping Time, Religiously . . . So to Speak

Beyond the practical discipline of self-evaluation and list-making, there's the deeper question: The use of time has aspects of a *spiritual* discipline.

Monks' days are strictly ordered, following a set rhythm of work and worship, solitude and communal activity, all signaled by the bells tolling the "canonical hours." Everything they do, including the schedules they keep, is done to the glory of God. "Why are we talking about monks?" you ask.

Visiting a monastery is a wonderful soul-nourishing activity. My husband and I visited a Trappist abbey in Iowa. It was a rambling group of old buildings, set way back in the midst of a cornfield, down a long tree-lined drive that made me think of the Europe I've never seen. Pastures and quietude surrounded the buildings. Meadowlarks called. I've heard it said that if you stand in a cornfield and listen closely, you can hear the whisper of the corn growing. I stood there and soaked in the murmur of the Midwest on a sunny, clear afternoon in July.

Inside was the indefinable smell that permeates old buildings—a mixture of ancient wood, musty corners, and waxed floors. And in this case, some incense, too. We bought bread at the gift shop, talked with the one monk who was permitted to speak to outsiders, dined in the refectory, and went to the chapel at the precisely appointed time to hear the monks singing psalms and Gregorian plainsong.

As they say: Nice place to visit, but ... I don't think I could live the regimented life of these devoted men.

Still, imagine concentrating your whole life to glorifying God—forsaking all worldly temptations and entanglements. You've got to admit that such order and simplicity, in today's overstuffed world, has some appeal.

HANDS ON

I know a family who is packing up to move to a 150-year-old log cabin in the foothills outside Seattle. Their reasons for the move are many, but one that struck me was the husband's desire to work with his hands—cutting wood, fixing up the cabin, making apple cider. He's spent years in international relief work, an area in which it's often hard to see "results," and he wants to make things, create things.

There's something deeply satisfying about working with your hands to make things that are both beautiful and useful. Have you ever thought about stripping and refinishing an old piece of furniture? Taking a ceramics class? Learning stenciling, calligraphy, or rosemaling? The point is to create something not only practical, but beautiful, something that gives you a tangible sense of accomplishment.

Is there anything that we modern, too-busy women, can learn from those who have renounced the world? We might consider recovering the idea of "canonical hours," specific hours for specific things, in our own lives.

Dallas Willard, in his book *Spirit of the Disciplines*, speaks of the disciplines that "deeply and essentially involve bodily conditions and activities": *solitude, fasting, celebration, service*, among other pursuits. He does not directly mention use of time, though the idea is there.

Why don't we commit our use of time to God?

Consider how you can use your time in ways that are pleasing to God. If He has endowed us with certain gifts, surely we shouldn't waste or deny those talents. Isn't it likely that He would want us to spend a certain amount of time cultivating them? We would also do well to learn to appreciate the beauty of His creation, set aside time to enjoy it, become attuned to seeing, hearing, and sensing it as an integral part of our world. And, we must be good stewards of the body He has given us. This includes *rest*.

Thankfully Yours

Then there are the everyday, repetitive tasks that can sometimes feel like the curse of Adam. I have a plaque above my kitchen sink with a prayer of Brother Lawrence:

O Lord of all pots and pans and things,
since I've not time to be a saint
by doing lovely things
or watching late with Thee . . .
Make me a saint by getting the meals
and washing up the plates.
Although I must have Martha's hands,
I have a Mary mind,
and when I black the boots and shoes,
Thy sandals, Lord, I find.

I love this simple, homely reminder that God is present in all we do, if we invite Him to be.

We've lived in four different homes, and that plaque is always the first thing to go up in my kitchen. It's always above the sink to remind me that even chores like scrubbing an egg-encrusted pan or sweeping up dog kibble from the kitchen floor can be performed in a spirit of service and devotion. Thank you, Lord, for two hands to "black the boots." Thank you for providing carrots and potatoes to make a stew. Thank you for a family to eat the stew and enjoy it with me.

MAKING SUNDAY A REAL DAY OF REST

If you've been involved in a particular church responsibility for a number of years, such as teaching Sunday school, it may be time to give yourself a sabbatical to "rest and renew the land." Could you hand over your duties to someone else for a couple of weeks? Could you use this time for quiet worship at home?

One man decided to take Sundays off from church for a few weeks. "Nothing's wrong," he told his pastor, "I just need some Sundays with my boys." He took his young sons to the river to skip stones and simply enjoy being together. He also brought along a radio so they could listen to a sermon. Then, on the way home, he asked his sons questions about the sermon.

For Christians actively involved in their church, Sundays can be less than restful. We should not neglect worship, but there are other ways to express praise and thanks to God.

After deciding to commit the use of our time to pleasing God, we must give our days and weeks a rhythm, and it begins with Sabbath-keeping. A pastor's wife told me this is difficult for them. Their Sundays are not a true sabbath. Her husband has Mondays off, but she works. I pointed out to her that the overriding sense of the commandment is a regular break in our schedules for rest and worship. I told her she could set aside an afternoon a week as her own sabbath. She said she would try.

In this age of workaholism, phones on airplanes and in cars, round-the-clock TV, all-night supermarkets, we need more than ever a time *set apart*. Even the sports and growing seasons overlap and run together—hockey in June, fresh tomatoes in January—so that we've lost the sense of "to everything there is a season."

Some of you may be shouting "legalist" about now, but keeping a sabbath makes great sense. If you work all week, taking a clean break from it all on Sunday makes sense for your spirit as well as your body. If you buy and consume all week, doesn't it seem sensible to refrain from that at least one day a week? If you drive to work every day, even leaving the car in the garage on Sunday (except for driving to church) gives you and your vehicle a break. We all need to "sit and rest a spell."

I look forward to Sundays. I prepare for it on Saturday night. I give my daughter her bath, and retire early myself. There's a comforting sense about this kind of ritual—something important to prepare for and look forward to.

Rhythms of Richness

Regular schedules add a sense of peace and security to our lives. For me, I anticipate Tuesday staff meetings, Wednesday night club at church, Thursday's trip to the farmers' market, reading the comics on Sunday afternoon. Put rhythm in your weeks, months; spread activities and duties out whenever possible, so they don't all bunch together. Consider adding others: a regular breakfast commitment, a Bible study, a facial or manicure.

Don't underestimate the refreshing rhythm of the seasons: the first corn-on-the-cob of summer, basking in the sun; selecting gourds and pumpkins in the fall, raking leaves; watching the first snowfall, sitting by a cozy fire; the return of robins in spring, the budding and blooming of trees and flowers. Observing the gifts of each season adds a depth and richness to life, to the humdrum. They speak to us of change and renewal, of God and His great love and care for us.

Cultivating good habits, disciplines, and rhythm to our daily lives soothes the spirit, rejuvenates the body, and removes the guilt and tension of the too-much-to-do, and when-am-I-going-to-do-it syndrome.

Our Connection to Life Itself

One of the most important activities we can commit ourselves to is prayer. Ask God to help you use your time wisely. Shoot up arrow prayers before plunging into a particularly challenging task. While you work, use meditative prayers that focus you on His abiding presence. At the end of every day you can look back and thank God for work accomplished, respite enjoyed—or you can merely express your gratitude that He got you through one of those out-of-control days.

I'm reminded of the need to pray for on-the-spot patience as Amanda interrupts me now to mediate for her in yet another dispute between her and a playmate. We're going to look at kids next—after I go help Amanda get her roller skates back.

4

How to Be the Perfect Mother and Other Big Laughs

AHA! Got your attention with that one, didn't I?

I suspect there's no area that induces more guilt in women than mothering. There's no area where we feel more inadequate, less equipped. Forget the avalanche of parenting advice we're buried under. We stumble, we pray, we cry. We run away from the specter of some perfect Christian role model (Shirley Dobson would never have given her kids a third Reese's Peanut Butter Cup and rationalized that peanut butter has protein.)

It's sad that we carry guilt about child-raising, because kids are great—and the guilt can sometimes blind us as to how much fun they really are! Before we look at the "guilt biggies," before we stare down the Perfect Mother and put her in her place, I want to tell you a story about a June evening with my daughter. And I want you to think about times you've had with your kids, when everything seemed so right. . . .

Magic in the Air

It was one of those magic summer evenings when the light fills the sky until late, and you don't want to come in because something in you wants to hold on to the moment as long as you can. You know that, soon enough, you will look out the window as you're doing the dinner dishes and you'll think, *My, it's starting to get dark early*. Mornings will hold a chill . . . and then it's January again. So, like dwellers in sub-arctic lands, we were making the most of the mid-summer light. Fireflies, those twinkling little stars of the meadow, were signaling. My child's playmates had all gone inside. But the wearying, drawn-out routine of coaxing her toward bed held no appeal for me. She could sleep in to-morrow.

We played ponies. Like Adam, we named the animals in our care—except these were plastic. We called them Spar-kle, Cherry, Snowflake, and Princess. Then we divided them into families according to certain categories. All this pony taxonomy took awhile—long enough for the light to fade. I stood up, with reluctance, and took my daughter and the various extended pony families inside, where we stabled them for the night. *So this is quality time*, I thought.

My play with Amanda normally consists of pushing her on the tire swing, taking her for walks, reading to her, and playing ball. We even just sit and talk on occasion, but I don't do a lot of the serious, get-on-the-floor kind of play like building forts with cushions, or having doll tea parties. It's hard to make polite conversation with a vacant-staring Barbie doll. But this time I was really getting into Aman-da's play, into her world.

We laughed a lot. It did not feel like an obligation. Only an hour or so on a summer's evening—but it meant so much to my little girl . . . and to me.

We need to hold on to those times. In our emotional account they balance out those nights when a child gets up four times after being put to bed—as Amanda did recently. That night I didn't feel like a particularly wonderful parent. I handled it badly, in fact. The parenting books assume that the world of children is rational and well-ordered, and rarely mention such nights. They give the impression that the right consistent formula will win out every time—and good mothers don't sit sobbing over their failures.

WHO'S THE REAL EXPERT?

I was talking with a friend of mine who is considering writing a book on parenting. She was concerned that a publisher might not be interested because she's not an expert. "Stop right there," I said, "You are an expert. You're in the trenches as a mother. That makes you an expert."

Have you lost confidence in your own mothering? Who knows more about your child than you do? Some of the best parents are those who trusted God and their own instincts—period. Too much advice, much of it conflicting, confuses us and makes us feel guilty. That's why I appreciate Dolores Curran (Stress and the Healthy Family). She writes a magazine column in which she answers readers' questions about childrearing. Very often, when a parent asks, "What should I do about this problem?" she'll reply, "Don't worry about it."

Now that's the kind of expert advice I like!

As you and I know, this simply is not the case. Kids are unpredictable, sometimes uncontrollable. For every quiet evening playing with ponies, there is a night when you get to the point of saying, "Okay, *you* stay up. *I'm* going to bed. Remember to turn out the lights and put out the cat."

"MOM!"

Let's say that you are feeling fairly at peace with who you are and where God has led you. Let us further assume that you have been able to arrive at some solutions as to how you order your time. You've begun to find the hand-holds that will pull you out of life's guilt traps.

Then you hear: *"MO-OMMM!"*

Mothering is an on-going role and obligation no matter what age your children are. Is it possible to be a conscientious, caring mother without wanting to run away from home? (I sure hope so.)

No mom is an island, but sometimes we need to be on one.
—Charlene Ann Baumbich

Seriously, friends, we need to come to terms with two stressors: *parental guilt* and *lack of control*.

What is your sure-fire guilt inducer? Here's a checklist of several possibilities:

- Letting your kids eat sugar.
- Letting your kids stay up too late.
- Letting your kids watch too much TV (including videos).
- Letting your kids do all three of the above at the same time.
- Barking "Because I said so" at your kids.
- Not forcing your teens to join the church youth group.
- Being inconsistent.
- Not listening to your mother or mother-in-law.
- Reading parental advice books.
- Not spending enough time with your kids.

Does any of that sound familiar? Parents have more things they feel guilty about than a church cookbook has recipes using cream of mushroom soup.

Right now, it's late evening and my daughter is playing outdoors. Do I let her play, and feel guilty about another late night? Do I call her in, and feel guilty about taking her away from her friends? Is it selfish of me to even worry about my own guilt? Why am I still trying to get this mothering business right after eight years? (I can hear parents of teens saying, "I'm still trying to get it right after *eighteen* years!")

Parental guilt is a close cousin of "being-guilt"—as in, "I am not *being* a good mother if. . . ." And also a cousin of "doing-guilt"—as in, "I should probably be *doing* more with/for my kids."

Most women are haunted by the specter of the Perfect Mother. She rattles her chains at midnight when we wake up with all those little worries that loom large at 3:00 A.M. The Perfect Mother is always cheerful. The Perfect Mother is fair, but firm. The Perfect Mother is in control. The Perfect Mother never whines—and she doesn't let her kids get away with it, either. The Perfect Mother actually does those "101 Activities for a Rainy Day" crafts—as opposed to sitting children in front of *Beauty and the Beast* for the fifty-seventh time. The Perfect Mother watches for sales on kids' clothes and school supplies and is always stocked up as opposed to having to run to the 7-Eleven store on a Sunday night and pay a king's ransom for notebook paper and pencils. The Perfect Mother always says yes when the Scouts, PTA, and athletic booster clubs come calling. . . .

The world stops for dirty diapers. —Anonymous

The Perfect Mother is a pain in the neck to deal with.

And she seems to be everywhere. We always have a sister or neighbor or friend who (we think) comes much closer to the ideal than we do. More seriously, you can't laugh her off. We all want desperately to do right by our kids, for our kids, even at great cost to ourselves.

When Amanda was an infant, she was a frequent night-waker. I was one of those breast-feeding purists who believed nothing but mother's milk would do for my darling: Not a drop of formula crossed my child's lips. Consequently, no one else could feed her. Breast-fed babies sup more frequently than those on bottles . . . and Amanda was on the small side anyway, so she was always hungry . . . and I was always awake, or so it seemed. Her pediatrician rewarded me with a comment on how healthy she was: "Good solid tissue," he said approvingly, thumping her on the back. "That's what comes from nursing."

"Great," I yawned.

In some misguided way, in the back of my mind the phrase kept recurring: "I must decrease so she can increase." And did I ever decrease. My husband and I hardly ever went out. I spent a lot of time holding my baby because somewhere I had read that American mothers should follow the example of African women and not coldly park their infants in cribs and playpens, but keep them on their physical person at all times. I felt noble in my self-sacrifice.

The problem with thinking that "I must decrease so she can increase," is that I am not the John the Baptist and Amanda is not the Christ. Also, I am more than a mother. I am a wife, I am a homemaker, I am a writer. . . . (And if I ever have another baby, my shelves will be stockpiled with cans of formula.)

Putting Parenting Into Perspective

To put parental guilt in its place, we have to *separate ourselves* from our children. Let me explain.

First, we must realize that our children are not miniature replicas of ourselves. Amanda is more than, other than, simply my daughter. Her athletic prowess, her uncanny interest in bugs, her skill in mathematics, and her beautiful straight hair have nothing to do with my parenting; they may not have anything to do with my genes.

The best parenting advice I ever heard was this: Study your children. Learn what makes them tick, what makes them cry. Explore the terrain of their God-given souls. Get to know them as delightful people in their own right—not as extensions of you and your attempts at being a Perfect Mother. Know that they will make mistakes, and allow them this freedom.

We've all heard of parents who "did all the right things" and their children still had behavior problems. That's really tough. But parenting isn't necessarily cause and effect. Your kid isn't *necessarily* having tantrums because you've gone back to work. He may just have a temper he needs to learn to control. You may have read the Bible every night to your children and taken them to church every Sunday. Now that they're teenagers they're not interested in going to church or reading their Bible. *Don't blame yourself.* They are making some choices of their own. It is in the province of faith to trust that, if you've laid a good foundation, they'll come back in time.

Second, we separate ourselves from our children by asserting our own human needs. I tell Amanda when I'm tired, for instance. It may not mean much to her now, but she'll learn eventually that I need sleep, too. If I am talking to a friend on the phone, I may ask Amanda to make her own snack. I need contact with other adults. This is not selfishness, it's self-preservation.

Contrarily, the Perfect Mother has no personal needs whatsoever. I'm always suspicious when I read someone's sentimental reminiscence about his mother, and he says something like, "She was never too busy to listen to us, never too busy to get down on the floor and play Chinese checkers with us." Either this woman had full-time servants, or no interests of her own. On the other hand, I'm always beguiled when someone talks about her mother like this: "She wasn't like anyone else's mother. She ran around in old painting smocks and liked to sculpt endangered species and make up crazy limericks." There's a woman I'd like to meet!

There *is* indeed such a thing as over-parenting—too much well-intentioned mothering—especially in this day and age when there's such a premium placed on *relating* to our children. Sometimes Amanda will tell me something that happened at school, and I will sit down with her in an effort to empathize, and say, "How did you feel when she said that?" Sometimes she'll toss her head with irritation and say, "Mom, I don't know!" The message is clear: Back off. I'll tell you in my own good time.

The Perfect Mother doesn't understand that.

We would do ourselves and our kids a favor to remember: *All parents, even the idealized Christian versions, make mistakes, aren't perfect, and are sometimes lazy.* In short, why can't we chill out? Why do Christians have to carry an extra burden of guilt here?

You know as well as I do all the things we're supposed to do: Watch for the teachable moments; volunteer in soup kitchens with our kids; conduct family devotions. Christian books and magazines are chockablock with meaningful family activities and other things we're *supposed* to do. If you did all those worthy things, you wouldn't have time to earn a living, sleep, eat, or floss.

I say it's more important to look at the big picture:

- Are you there for your children when they really need you?
- Do you communicate God's love to them?
- Do you enjoy their company? Do they enjoy yours?
- Are they reasonably healthy, well-fed, clothed, and housed? (Messy rooms don't count.)

Why worry if you allow them an occasional *Twinkie*—or if you sometimes utter a discouraging word. You know your child. Trust yourself. Trust your kid. Most of all, trust God. In the end, your children really belong to Him.

The "C" Word

Now for a word about *control*, or lack of same.

It's a summer morning, and you're leaving on vacation in a couple of days. You have one or two things to do: Stop the mail, take the dog to the kennel, pay a couple of bills, wash clothes and pack, take the car in for a tune-up. You've gotten up early so as to get a good start on the day. The first load of laundry is already in the cycle, you've made a couple of phone calls, you're in the process of cleaning house. (At least that's what I always do before going out of town. I guess I don't want the burglars to see any dust.) Nine o'clock goes by . . . nine-thirty . . . and still no sound from your child's bedroom.

You get restless. You need to get going, and get the car in to the shop. Finally, as you're scrubbing the toilet, she comes out rubbing her eyes. "Mommy, my stomach hurts."

And then . . . up it comes. All over her. All over you. All over the rug. All over your carefully laid plans.

Smothering an urge to scream or sob, you clean her up and put her in a fresh nightgown. No fever. Maybe it's one of those twenty-four-hour bugs. "Back to bed with you, young lady."

You call the garage and explain that you won't be bringing the car in this morning. Maybe your husband can come home early and bring it in. Meanwhile, there's nothing to do about it but wait. It's not your child's fault, poor kid. At least you can get the housecleaning done, you tell yourself. But as you run the vacuum cleaner in the living room you feel your head starting to throb. . . .

If you only knew how early I started to get here this late.
—Mother of preschoolers

No one ever said children were convenient. If it's not sickness, it's balkiness when you're rushing to get ready for work. They forget to tell you about a school science project until five on Sunday afternoon, and the project requires finding ten samples of mosses and lichens. You have to go searching in the woods for this stuff—and it's raining.

There are four words to remember when you get the feeling that things are out of control. Humor, Flexibility, Point-of-View (the child's), and Perspective.

You've no doubt seen the *Family Circus* cartoon showing Billy's route from point A to point B, traced by a tortuous broken line. He backtracks, takes side trips, jumps over things, stops to pet a dog—anything but the shortest distance between the two points. Kids don't think like we do. They don't understand about planning ahead; they aren't strapped to a specific time frame. For them, the world is full of delightful diversions. I may be rushing to get to the post office before it closes, but Amanda is more interested in watching an army of ants attempt to jam a deceased earthworm down a hole. You've got to admit the ants are more intriguing.

Perspective gets us through a lot. Someday we may have the peace and quiet and well-managed schedules we always dreamed about. That will be when the pink and blue ponies will have long since been led off to the garage sale corral, and no crying, thirsty, sick children will be waking us up in the middle of the night.

The next phase will be grandparenting, when we can enjoy all the fun and none of the guilt.

All this to say—hang in there, good mother! There's lots to look forward to.

5
The State of Your Unions

SOMETHING REALLY NEAT happened to me recently. I had a "friend day."

First, my former boss took me out to lunch at a Chinese restaurant. It was fun to talk ideas with Harold while I dipped pieces of shellfish into sweet-and-sour sauce; to feel back-in-the-loop for an hour or so.

When I returned home, no one was there. I had three or four free hours to fill before my family returned. What to do? Write? Nah. Housework? I was caught up, and wondering how that had happened. I called Diane. "Is this a good time?" I asked.

"Sure," she said. "In fact, I was thinking about giving you a call today."

"Well, how *are* you?" I asked, settling into a chair. . . .

Ninety minutes later, I had found out how she was, and she had found out how I was. Her child was asleep. No one had interrupted—as so often happens when we try to engage in a conversation of more than perfunctory content. Nor did we feel guilty!

I can't believe how good that felt. And it wasn't over yet—my friend day.

Later, I was puttering in my office, doing something with file folders, when the doorbell rang. I wasn't expecting anyone. Usually someone at the door is collecting money for this or that, or a neighbor kid wants to play with Amanda. People just don't drop in these days, at least not where I live.

But there was Charlene. "I was just on my way home from the dentist and I'm all swollen from root-canal work and I thought I'd stop by."

Maybe you're reading this and thinking, *Great for her. She has all these people in her life. She has time for these relationships. But I can count my true friends on one hand. Everyone in my church is over fifty. I have to work ten hours a day. I'm stuck at home with small children and can't afford baby-sitters, and all the other women in my neighborhood work. We moved a year ago and I still haven't been able to make connections. I'm a single parent and feel left out by others.*

Or maybe you're saying, *I have friends and wish I didn't! They're always calling me with their problems, asking me to do favors for them, and I never get anything in return. I feel like they tear me down in subtle ways. After I'm with them I feel empty and I don't know why.*

Let me tell you something: This day was *a rarity*, believe me.

More typical is a week where I might have one lunch, a few hurried phone calls, some brief conversations at church. And more often are the days I sit at home, all by myself, working alone. I wonder if anyone cares, and if there is intelligent life out there beyond the demands of parenthood, and whether I can persuade some publisher to send me to Vermont to do a book on Christian bed-and-breakfast proprietors.

Sometimes I read articles in which the writer relates some wonderful conversation between she and a friend in a quaint tea room, or how she led someone to Christ aboard a cross-country flight, and I think, *Why doesn't that happen to me?* I see photos in women's magazines of well-dressed friends laughing on a park bench, and I think, *Get real! Where are their kids? Why are these women so perfectly dressed and coiffured?* I mean, have you and your friend hung out in a park lately in one-hundred-and-fifty-dollar Icelandic sweaters?

THROW OUT THOSE RANCID EMOTIONS

Of course you're careful not to voice criticism. Most of us spend a lot of effort trying to tame our tongues! But what about taming our thoughts? The late Catherine Marshall LeSourd once talked about the discipline of "doing a fast on criticism." It's so easy to slip into critical thoughts about other people, even people we care about. Over several days, keep a record of the number of times a critical thought enters your mind. You don't have to write it down; but be aware of it. Then ask God to help you become more compassionate, more empathetic, less judgmental. You might even ask a trusted friend to hold you accountable to keep this "fast."

To replace critical thoughts, think of people you're close to and list their good traits, including qualities you would like to emulate. What you're really doing is throwing out the rancid emotions of jealousy, envy, and a critical spirit, and working on a "re-seasoning" of your attitudes toward others.

Given the usual state of my life, my "friend day" has stayed with me a long time. I really needed that.

It's true that we cannot care for ourselves, stretch ourselves, grow in Christ, if we are all alone. We were created for fellowship with others. True friends make us *more* of what God intended us to be. They teach us lessons in un-

59

selfishness. They extend our world. They bring lightness and diversion into our lives. They can even *change* us.

That's when friendship works.

What if we don't have enough friends? What if our friends let us down? What if we're feeling guilty because we haven't kept in touch with someone who needs us? Where do we find the time?

The One True Friend

I know what it's like to be really lonely. During my adolescence I believed I was *The Loneliest Person in the World*. I was almost proud of it, thinking of myself as a friendless, solitary *artiste*—the creative soul so sensitive that no one could possibly understand me. They were going to proms and pep rallies . . . I was sitting at home in my room.

I wasn't happy. I'd sure do it differently if I had the chance to do it over. But I also see that it was a time of learning and observing, a time of laying foundations.

Nearly everyone has been lonely at one time or another in their lives, even people we think of as busy and popular. You may know a lonely person and not even realize it—we get pretty adept at covering it up. You may be lonely. To that I respond: First, you can use this time to grow; second, it will pass; third, there is Someone out there who would like to get to know you.

Often, Christ comes to us when we are lonely or needy. It is then that we can hear Him more clearly, respond to Him more readily. It happened to me that way—I received Christ at a time when I had no job, no friends, no prospects. I was spending a lot of time reading authors like C. S. Lewis, searching for a deeper meaning to my life. I couldn't have put it into words at the time, but I was longing for Christ. And what Christ was saying to me was something like this: "You may be feeling separated from other people right now, but before you can connect with them you have to connect with Me. Seek my kingdom first, and everything else will follow."

At the time, I didn't know the "right" words to pray to ask Jesus to come into my life. It was more of an incoherent, profound desire: *Come, Lord Jesus!*

And He did. Gradually, I became aware of His presence in my life.

The Bible reveals a God who longs for fellowship with His people. David puts it this way: "[The Lord] brought me out into a spacious place; he rescued me because he delighted in me" (Psalm 18:19). If you're already a Christian, even if you're feeling lonely right now, you're a giant step ahead of where I was in my stumbling quest. You know how to pray. You are familiar with the promises in God's Word. God is a part of your life, and as long as He is, you can't be truly lonely.

So, if circumstances have put you in a place where you don't have as many friends as you would like, maybe it's time to turn to God. From the tone of it, some of the most profound devotional literature was created out of loneliness. *Write down your reflections. Read a good devotional book. Read the Psalms.* When I've been lonely, good books have been faithful companions. If there are contemporary Christian authors who have helped you, write to them—most will be delighted to hear from you! (I love getting mail.) And pray, not only that God will send people into your life, but that He will equip *you* to reach out to others, including those who don't know Him.

There have also been times when my husband and I were not really lonely, but dissatisfied with the state of our friendships. We were in the pastorate for a number of years, and the demands of the church pretty much filled up our social calendar so that we didn't have time to cultivate many relationships. Unfortunately, when we left pastoring, we were left without a lot of close friends. It has taken several years to build new connections, and we're still working on them.

Are You Out of It?—Or in the Path?

Loneliness passes, and sometimes you simply have to wait it out—and, while you're waiting, try to do everything you can to put yourself in the path of new friends.

I once participated in a panel on friendship for a magazine article. One of the things we agreed on was the fact that friendship takes more time than most of us realize. We can expect too much of other people—who are also busy with their own concerns and schedules and can be obtuse about another's needs. We're probably not going to be invited for Sunday dinner the first time we visit a church. If we move into a new neighborhood, we probably won't be greeted with homemade bread and offers to baby-sit our children.

It's taken four years—from one Olympics to the next, an entire presidential term—for my husband and me to get to the place where we feel close to the inner circle of our church, where I can honestly say I have good friends in the congregation. Even in our church, which is fairly homogeneous, people have trouble connecting. It is *not* easy.

But you've got to start. Someone has to make the first move. Put yourself in the path of potential friends. Try that new study or discussion group—or offer to start one. Invite someone to lunch or out to coffee. Don't wait to be asked—ask.

Not everyone has to be "our kind" to qualify as a potential friend. I've seen some wonderful inter-generational friendships, for example. And we can—indeed, we are commanded to—reach out in Christian love to unbelievers or seekers. But our likelihood of making connections increases if we have a larger "pool" of possible friends to draw from. This could be through professional networks, a spiritually and socially compatible church, volunteer organizations, twelve-step groups, even with your extended family if you live in the same area.

Here's the thing: Other people are looking for the same

friendship opportunities. The women's section in my Sunday paper has an amazingly long list of groups, complete with phone numbers and contact persons. Groups for Christian businesswomen. Groups for overeaters. Groups for political activists. Groups for the recently widowed. What does this proliferation tell us but that there is widespread longing for deep relationships?

Does all this sound calculating, as if I'm leaving out God's providence? No: As I look at my friendships, I can see God's hand behind every one of them. I had no idea when I agreed to speak at a writers' conference, that Charlene would come up to me and introduce herself. I had no idea when I went to work at my last job, that the company president and I would discover we had a lot in common and enjoy just shooting the breeze by the coffee station.

But you see, *I put myself in the path of these God-made surprises.* I didn't sit at home, hoping someone would magically find out I was alive and decide to make my acquaintance because somehow they knew I was a wonderful human being. (That's what I used to do.)

If you're feeling lonely, or want to expand your circle of friends, know this: Someone out there needs you. Don't get so wrapped up in yourself and your immediate concerns that you miss these signals. I say this out of experience— the experience of having shyness misinterpreted as snobbishness, the experience of assuming that no one wanted to know me, the experience of setting up false barriers between me and others.

Take a risk—make a friend. Remember when you were a kid and your mother would say to you, "Why don't you make friends with that nice Susie Jones down the street?" You probably thought, *That "nice" Susie Jones? If she only knew!* But as usual, Mom had a point. (I find myself saying the same thing to my daughter and being greeted with resounding apathy.) You can't always wait for the serendipitous spark to ignite. If you find someone interesting, you have to persist, invite them over . . . and be patient.

If grownup Susan Jones down the street is not—as far as you know—a Christian, you may wonder, *What do I have in common with this unsaved woman?* Look past surface differences. Sure, she may smoke or drink or do brunch on Sunday mornings. But you may be surprised what you have in common to talk about.

I have a close friend whose neighbor is not a Christian, not even a lapsed or nominal believer. But they enjoy each other's company, their toddlers play together (as much as toddlers do anything "together") and their husbands get along. My friend is praying that God will open doors to tell her neighbor about the love of Christ—but in the meantime, she's *showing* her neighbor the love of Christ.

Tending Your Friendships

Okay. Now you have all these scintillating, inspiring, supportive friends. Now what?

Having friends is a little like having planted a vegetable garden. The vegetables look wonderful on the seed packet, and you love the idea of all that fresh produce once it's harvested, but then there's all this weeding and watering and thinning and fertilizing you have to do. You've got to tend friendships, and sometimes that means dealing with thistles and nettles.

Here are some ways I've hurt my friends:
- Not called when they were sick.
- Betrayed confidences, unintentionally.
- Been competitive.
- Haven't answered letters.
- Had negative thoughts about them.

Nice, huh? Of course, I've had most of the same things done to me, and so have you. Friendships are complicated. They take time and energy. We need to ask ourselves: *How important is this relationship to me?: Am I growing in Christ through this relationship? Does this friendship fill my tank or drain it? How do I feel when I've been with this person?*

THE STATE OF YOUR UNIONS

IS THE WEIGHT OF YOUR FRIENDS ON YOUR SHOULDERS?

Our friendships can weigh us down more than we realize. Do you sometimes feel that you're bearing the brunt of your friends' complaints, concerns, neediness? Are they doing the same for you? What's the tone of your conversations with them? Do they tend to be serious, even painful?

You may be making yourself too emotionally available. Try tracking your interactions with your friends over a given period of time, maybe a month or two. Make a mental note of which exchanges are heavy, which are light and fun, and which are somewhere in between. (Or, if you're really ambitious, you could write them down.) If you find your friendships are skewed to the weighty, you might try shedding that burden by asking your friend if she's tried to solve her problem another way ("Have you talked this out with your husband?")

For further insight on the one-sided friendship, I recommend Getting Beyond "How Are You?" by David Mains and Melissa Mains Timberlake, which contains an excellent chapter on "Questions I Wish Others Would Ask Me."

We like to think all relationships are important, all friendships equally worthy of our attention. But one of the crazymakers for most of us is overcommitment. Too much involvement can make us feel like we want to run away from it all. We've got to be realistic, even a little hard-nosed, about the friendship question.

For instance, you may be a person who prefers *fewer but deeper friendships*, long one-on-one conversation, strong spiritual bonds. If this is what nurtures and replenishes you, you may really need only two or three good friends (and in any case those really deep relationships are hard to come by). Any more would stretch your ability to give these relationships the level of commitment you prefer. And most likely—it would drain you dry.

Or maybe the *shape of your life* dictates the shape of your relationships. Let's say you have a lot of kids, or you work a lot of overtime or late-night hours. Or you have an aging relative who needs your attention. You just don't have the time or energy to sustain a lot of friendships at this point in your life. This will change, but right now it's a given you have to work with.

Expectations

What do you *expect* from your friendships? Frequent get-togethers, many meaningful conversations, time to hang out? You may need to revise your expectations.

My mother's best friend, back in the 50s, lived next door. They were both at home with young kids and saw each other all the time. The two dads commuted to work together. It was like Lucy and Ricky and Fred and Ethel on the *I Love Lucy* TV show. But things are different now. In today's suburban sprawl, good friends may be an hour away by freeway. Work schedules conflict: You may be a teacher who's off at four, but your best friend, a nurse in an intensive care unit, works nights and weekends and wants to be with her kids the rest of the time. People move. Things change.

Yesterday, I spent more than two hours on the phone with a friend who lives in another state. In the morning. At full rates (I called her). But, you see, we go several months between conversations, so when we do talk we make the most of it. Eileen is a relatively new friend, and we're discovering all sorts of delightful things we have in common. You, too, may have more "long-distance friends" than you realize. Don't write them off—*write to them!* Sometimes a periodic, long phone call or a letter is just enough.

Do you expect every acquaintance to flower into something deeper? They don't have to. Friendships can be light, or casual. There are a few mothers at school who fall into this category for me. I enjoy seeing them around the neighborhood and at school events, but I haven't sought a deeper friendship, because these connections fill a certain need: They're pleasant and undemanding, and in these harried times anything that's undemanding is a welcome relief.

Do you expect friends to reciprocate every phone call and invitation and feel disappointed when they don't? I have a couple of friendships like that. I put more energy into them than the other guy does. I'm the one who initiates the contact. Sometimes I've wondered if the other person really cares, and why am I wasting my time? But they do care. In these relationships, I'm the one who has a little more time and energy, so I give of myself—and get something back.

Do you expect every friendship to last forever? There are times when a relationship fills a specific need we might have at a certain time in our life—then our circumstances change and we move on, and we let the relationship wither. We might be in a new mothers' group with other new moms. We talk about breast-feeding and lack of sleep and swap baby-care books. Then our kids grow up and the group disbands, because the babies were what kept us together. Maybe you grew close to a co-worker while both of you were involved in a demanding assignment on the job— but once the deadlines were met you drifted apart. That's inevitable . . . and it's okay.

The Takers

If you have close friends you see regularly or even occasionally, people who fill you up, help you grow, bring out the best in you—you are blessed. It's well worth making room in your life for these special friends.

Then there are those people who make us feel diminished. Friends who are always in need, or who demand more than you have to give.

Have you ever had the experience of concluding a conversation with someone you thought was a friend—only to realize she had subtly undermined your self-esteem? On further reflection you realize this happens a lot with this particular friend.

Or maybe there's someone you have breakfast with occasionally, and the last time you got together it came to you that she never asks how *you* are. It's all *her* life, *her* needs, *her* accomplishments.

There are others: the friend who lurches from crisis to crisis and never seems to pull her life together. The friend who uses you as a free therapist . . . or sitter . . . or chauffeur.

Some years ago I had a friend who struggled continually with just about everything. She went from job to job—and it was always her employer's fault that she left. She was always coming up with grandiose plans (*"Now* I'm going to get myself together") that never panned out. She made, I felt, a series of very wrong financial decisions. She even flirted with New Age philosophies, although she had been raised in the evangelical church.

At the time, I was struggling in some areas, too, so we were drawn to each other by our mutual pain. Let me tell you this is *not* the basis for a healthy friendship. But slowly—through God's graciousness and some careful planning on my part—my life started coming together. Hers did not. It unraveled further. I was changing, becoming more conservative in my values. She was disillusioned with the church. Finally, when I told her of my dream to write books, she scoffed, "It's impossible to get published. You'd have to work at it for at least five years." About eight months later I was signing my first book contract.

This friend was a negative energy drain for me. I found that I needed to protect myself spiritually. I suppose I could have made the effort to help her in that area—and yes, I feel guilty about it—but my armor wasn't in place a few years ago in the way that it is now. My need was, and still is, to connect with strong Christians whose example and counsel help equip me for the battle.

She's moved out of state now, and I sometimes wonder how she's doing. But I was the one who made the hard decision to let the relationship go in order to move on. I don't think I made the wrong decision. Sometimes it's the *only* decision.

Everything to Everyone

We women tend to have a problem "homing-in" on what's best for us—on God's best for us. We want to be everything to everyone, and we can't be. If a "friend" demeans you, demands excessive amounts of time, brings out the worst in you, you may need to be less available to that person, or even confront her in the spirit of Christian love.

You may need to come to terms with the idea that not every "friendship" is worth holding on to.

From time to time we all need to take stock of our friendships—assess the "state of our unions." Ask yourself: What's the state of my friendships? Am I holding up *my* end of the deal? Am I sometimes critical or carelessly hurtful? Am I letting myself be loved, making room in my life for someone who may need me? Am I having enough plain *fun* with my friends? Am I letting myself be run ragged by others? Am I satisfied with my level of intimacy? Are my friendships in tune with where my life is now? If I just don't have a lot of time to develop friendships right now, can I accept that? Can I be patient and trust God's leading as I seek out new friends?

Most of us aren't blessed with many "friend days" like the one I described at the beginning of this chapter. But there are many ways to find and *keep* those friendships that delight us and honor God. Even if we haven't spent much time on park benches or cross-country flights lately.

6
Yes, You Can Be Too Thin

THE PHONE RANG eleven times yesterday.

I know this because I started counting after call number eight. Two excessively long conversations with friends. Someone selling homeowners' insurance. A man from church wanting us to lead a small group during Lent. A speaking invitation. A lawn-care service: "We were out looking at your trees, and they need. . . ." (I hate the thought of strange men casing my property: "Haw, haw, Joe, look at that magnolia. It ain't gonna make it through the spring.")

Didn't these people know? I have to make cupcakes for school, prepare a message for our church women's retreat, write an article, pay the mortgage, talk to Amanda's teacher about her low-effort mark in math . . . And the thing is, I kind of like it that way. Well, most of the time.

Whether you're a work-at-home person like me, a pillar in the PTA, the mother of three preschoolers, a part-time or even full-time employee, the neighborhood mom who takes care of everyone else's kids, you know what I'm talking about: Women have to juggle a dozen things all at the

PUTTING MA BELL IN HER PLACE

The telephone, as most of you will agree, is an insidious time thief. Author Patricia Sprinkle offers these tips to make the phone serve you, not vice versa:

• When working on major projects, decide not to answer the phone for a time. Arrange to have calls forwarded to someone else (trade a morning of answering with a friend), use an answering machine, or take the phone off the hook.

• When you are busy and someone asks if you have a minute to talk, answer honestly but gently, "No, I'm afraid I don't right now." Set up a mutually convenient time to talk. When you call other people, make the habit of asking them if this is a convenient time to talk.

• Limit your calls. You might even post a sign near the phone: "Are you talking too long?"

• If you must make several calls in a row (an efficient way to use the telephone), list all the numbers in one place, so that if one number is busy or not answering, you can call later without looking up the number again.

• Keep a book or handwork near the phone for times when you are put on "hold."

• You don't have to have a car phone, portable phone, or call-waiting, simply because they are available. Decide how much space and time you want invaded by the telephone.

• Write elected officials urging a ban on telephone solicitation.

same time. Many of them are good things, maybe most of them are. But there are days when all these commitments put together can feel like too much of a good thing, like stuffing yourself at the dessert table. Sometimes you really long for celery sticks and austerity . . . or a house without a phone.

Why do we do this to ourselves? One answer is sitting right between your ears. It's your brain.

You and Your Big *Corpus Callosum*

Women have amazing brains. Now, I'm not a scientist, but I have read what the scientists say about the subject, and it makes sense to me: Researchers have found that the *corpus callosum*, the portion of the brain that connects the two hemispheres of it (I have a mental picture of a cranial Isthmus of Panama) is more developed in the female than in the male. Don't get excited. This does not mean that we are smarter than men (necessarily), but it *does* suggest why women are more apt to think about and do several things at a time, while men are more single-mindedly focused.

I have a phone with an extra long cord. When I'm talking, I walk around, doing odd jobs. I empty the dishwasher, wipe out the refrigerator, hang up towels in the bathroom. I can do all this and still complain to my mother or negotiate with a publisher. When my husband talks on the phone, which he rarely does voluntarily, he sits down and *talks* on the phone.

I drive him crazy because I talk in what seems to him like *non sequiturs* (unrelated fragments). "One thing at a time!" he pleads, as I rattle on about the day's schedule, the news, the weather, Amanda's field trip. Makes perfect sense to me. He, for some reason, prefers a logical flow of related subject matter. He zeroes-in on one target. I talk all over the map, picking up stray Barbie doll clothes as I go.

I can remember my dad saying to my mother (in an irritated voice), "Why don't you finish one thing before you start another?" Mom always seemed to leave a trail of distraction. The vacuuming would be half-done when she started to dust. The dust cloths would still be out while she started dinner. "I was going to finish, but I got sidetracked," was her classic explanation. Meanwhile, Dad would be out in the garden spading away for hours, not even stopping to eat.

In her own way, Mom got the job done, and I do, too. But . . . eleven phone calls?

It *is* possible to be too thin—or at least to be *spread* too thin. I took the phone calls, but I could have let the answering machine do what we pay it to do. How do we find the balance between healthy involvement and guilt-inducing over-commitment? Few of us would be willing to give up everything and be like Simeon Stylites, the reclusive early church father who dwelt atop a column in the desert. After all, God made our brains the way they are for a reason (probably so the eyes in the back of our head could watch the kids while we're cleaning up after the dog).

Most women really do best when they have a lot of variety in their lives. (The *corpus callosum* demands it to thrive.) But there *are* limits, and we need to know when we've reached them.

Reflect for a moment. How do you think of yourself? List the roles you play, the hats you wear, the things you do for the people you love. (Be positive.)

This is the list I've come up with:

- Christian, saved by God's grace in Jesus Christ
- Wife
- Mother
- Writer
- Speaker
- Homemaker
- Daughter
- Sister
- Committed member of a church body
- Friend

- Sometime school volunteer
- Reader
- Walker
- Bird lover

Make your own list. There probably aren't many roles on your list you would want to delete.

But think a little further. Beneath each role, mentally list the involvements and activities required by those roles. Now is there anything you could delete? If your packed schedule has gotten to the point where you're forgetting things, making crazy mistakes, and wondering when you fall into bed at night, *Did I really do anything of significance today?* it's probably time to take inventory and see what can be reasonably eliminated from your schedule to allow for what is important.

Otherwise what happens is we turn fifty, and the kids are gone and we look around and ask how much of it mattered to anyone, and where to now?

Trivia

Even as I write this I'm becoming distracted. I just heard the neighbor start his lawn mower. Now I'm thinking about our lawn. It's fall, and the leaves are starting to pile up, and neither Fritz nor I has had time to have a good "yard day" and get our acreage cleaned up in preparation for winter. I could dismiss the worry. After all, we both have work to do, and the lawn will simply have to wait. But it's hard to ignore the brain connection that causes my attention to wander between my computer and the yard.

This *mental noise* is a hidden stressor for women—all the interior planning, worrying, calculating. Most of us find it wearying and depleting. However, there are some of us who seem to gravitate *toward* that mental noise.

A friend told me about a woman who blows into her neighbor's house in a cloud of chaos. She is constantly distracted: "Omigosh, where'd I leave my checkbook?" She seems incapable of sitting still, being quiet, renewing her inner resources. Some women actually fear the quiet—afraid of what they might find there.

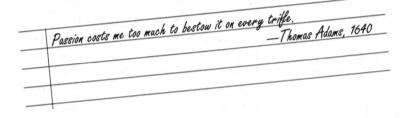

Passion costs me too much to bestow it on every trifle.
—Thomas Adams, 1640

What consumes your day? Meaningless activity—trivia? Are you afraid that if you slow down you won't know what to do with yourself? Can you turn off the mental noise and listen to the voices that matter?

First, recognize that God has built into you a need for variety. Rightly channeled, it's a good thing.

If you are working outside your home, it's okay not to want to spend *all* your time on your career. If you work full time and your life is feeling out-of-kilter because of the demands of your job, you may want to step back and analyze your situation. Could you afford to go part time? Change jobs? Work at home? Quit your job altogether?

If you work at home full time, it's also okay to want some freedom outside the home. You probably need more variety than you realize. Just because you are home doesn't mean you always have to be the school room parent, the den mother, the baby-sitter of everyone else's kids. It doesn't mean you aren't fulfilling your duty as a Christian woman if you don't do everything everyone else expects of you. You may want to rethink your situation. Could you work part time? Start a home business? Be a volunteer for something that especially appeals to you? Don't volunteer out of guilt.

Do what you would like to do and feel most comfortable with.

Stagnation

The challenge is to seek balance with meaning. While we don't want to juggle too much, we also don't want to reduce our life to one or two things. My good friend who is a musician spoke to me after church last Sunday. I was complaining about the activities that I thought stood between me and my writing. "Why do I take these on?" I asked.

"Because they keep you fresh," she said. "We'd get stale if we never did anything else but our work."

She had a point. Don't get so good at saying no to things that you say no to everything. Maybe we need to think in terms of what we say yes to.

There are some hard choices here. When I look at my list of roles and relationships, my commitments, it's clear that I enjoy most of this stuff—*but I don't enjoy it all equally*.

After you've cut the things you consider a poor use of time, like shopping as an end in itself, watching television for no particular reason, looking at magazines and catalogs until you are in a dreamy stupor . . . You may need to give your activities another round of cuts (like the politicians making another round of budget cuts).

If you have trouble determining what to say yes to, ask yourself these questions:

- What really matters to me?
- What fits with my gifts?
- Where do I feel God is leading me to minister?
- How much time do I *really* have for this?
- What will happen if I say no?

When I think in these terms, I'm more able, like Mary, to choose the "better portion." I feel led to helping women deepen their spiritual lives. I can do that through writing, speaking, certain church activities, and contact with friends. This matters to me and fits with my gifts, so I tend to concentrate my involvement in these areas.

A DIALOGUE

"Yes, Lord, I am forever tired in my efforts to . . . love. It is a full-time job. Sometimes my hands do not move heartily in the service of Your love. In fact, today my hands hang limp. I do not feel like doing anything. I am spent, depleted, washed up on shore like an empty shell.

"But my list is long! The Sunday school class needs teaching. The bathrooms need cleaning. The clothing needs ironing. An article is past deadline; and my neighbor is smarting from divorce. So much to do. So many to serve. So much harvest not yet in. . . ."

My child, come close. Put aside your list. I have built the fire. Come sit by Me. Nothing brings Me more delight than to love you. But sometimes, child, you seem to have a hard time letting Me love you. Love puts you in charge; receiving love means I am the giver and you are the taker. Doing love is high-profile; receiving love is what happens between you and Me in private.

I am not surprised that you are wearied by the doing of love. When you think you can do all the loving, you will get weary. When you cannot receive, you will soon have nothing to give.

If you love Me, yes, feed My lambs. But if you love Me, first be My lamb.

—Ruth Senter

Conversely, I don't especially enjoy purely social occasions. I like to have a *reason* to get together with people, whether it be professional, spiritual, or around some volunteer work. Doing lunch costs money, takes time (and puts on pounds). I've become selective about the social commitments I make. At the same time my friendships do matter to me, so I'm working on other ways to nurture them.

Reality Check

Like me, you probably need to give yourself periodic reality checks on how much time you can give to *anything* beyond the immediates of family, work, eating, and sleeping! There really are times when we need to hunker down, catch up around the house, guard our health by getting

YOU CAN SLOW DOWN THE CLOCK

Do you always seem to feel short of time? The surest way to slow down the clock may be to ignore it, says Geoffrey Godbey, Ph.D., author of *The Future of Leisure Services.* "The more we're aware of time's value, the scarcer time seems." The best way to erase time consciousness is through "activities that require some skill," like playing an instrument or a sport. "When you're completely absorbed," he says, "time isn't an issue."

more sleep. And there are times when we absolutely need to put our families first. (When was the last time you and your husband did something fun together?) There are times, and we can sense them, when our children need all of us, as opposed to part of us. (Isn't it remarkable how they know when Mom's distracted?)

It isn't always easy—as a letter I received today from a dear college friend attests. Ann was always the one who was going to go out and conquer the world. She was accepted at a prestigious graduate school and dreamed of a career in the State Department, or as an eminent professor. Today, three kids (one of them with a disability) and twenty years later, she's renewed her pursuit of a Ph.D. and is keeping her hand in by teaching occasional college classes. She writes, "I have made *some* progress on the dissertation. The truth is that having two teens and one preteen is a full-time job, as I've reluctantly acknowledged this year." But, she concludes, "all *will* be well."

Yes, it will.

We have to choose—in both the big and little things.

Sometime soon, look at your calendar. Write down the various commitments you're juggling right now. Then write down some things you'd like to be doing, including the fun, "just-for-me" things we all put on the back burner. What commitments could you eliminate, or commit to less frequently? If you have lunch with a friend every month, for example, could you make that every other month? Look at other things you do regularly, and see if you can do them less frequently. If you want to add something, like becoming involved in a serious Bible study once a week, you will obviously have to give up something else.

Or maybe you've discerned that you really prefer to concentrate your gifts and energies in *one* area, at least for a time. Don't feel guilty about dropping everything else in favor of that one thing.

I know this may sound *organized, pragmatic*. But organization has been known to save the sanity of many a stressed-out woman! Organization rooted in *meaning* is better yet. And we're going to go deeper into our search for meaning.

Meanwhile, enjoy your female brain—it's an amazing gift! But remember to give it a rest every now and then. Even those wonderful connections can get frayed with over-use.

7

On the Matter of Resourcefulness

ONE REASON WOMEN FEEL overloaded with activity is because we tend to soldier on alone. We try to do it all ourselves. As if, on the stone wall of womanhood, someone wrote the graffiti: *Never ask for help!*

I heard about a couple who had lived in their house for seven years. During that time, the master bedroom remained undecorated. After awhile, the husband was getting tired of the "empty warehouse" look, and the lack of progress on the decoration front was becoming a sore point. So one day the husband and wife sat down for a heart-to-heart. They had set aside the money, what was the hold-up? The wife admitted that she felt incompetent to decorate—to choose the right colors and fabrics and patterns. "Why don't you ask someone for help?" her understanding mate suggested.

The GECW Syndrome

We all have weak areas like that. Maybe you don't have an artistic eye either, and you wonder how a friend's home looks so great. Sometimes we deal with limited resources—

your husband has the car all the time and you're stuck at home with small children; your lawn mower is on its last wheels, and you're worrying about how you'll afford a replacement; you've been dealing with a family illness and there's no time to work on your income taxes.

You sense that the woods are teeming with people out there who can help you, but it's so hard to ask. Most often, we don't think we *should* be asking for help. This, I tell you, is part of a ghastly illness I have discovered, called "The Good Evangelical Christian Woman Syndrome." And too many of us, hereinafter referred to as GECW, suffer from it.

I know this: I have the dread disease myself. I hate to ask favors. My husband and I spend a lot of time *doing* for others. We chauffeur children to school. We help people move. We bring homemade soup to convalescing friends. I've counseled many beginning writers about breaking into print. We try to practice hospitality without expecting an invitation in return. And that doesn't even take into account our involvements at church and school. We've always believed we should live out our faith by doing for others. (Isn't there a chorus that goes, "And they'll know we are Christians by our casseroles . . ."?)

But learning to receive . . . aah, that's something else again. The "syndrome" kicks in.

People are too busy, I reason. *What can I do for them in return?* Then, *I hate to feel so needy. I should be more self-sufficient. What will people think of me?* Meanwhile, I run myself ragged doing everything myself; the house goes without needed repairs; and my husband and I stay home because "I can't" get a sitter.

When I do ask—even for a ride somewhere—I tend to hem and haw. Finally, in a tiny, apologetic voice I murmur, "Um, I have a favor to ask. I know it's out of your way, but could you possibly give me a lift to church. . . ?"

The usual response is a hearty, "Sure!" (But I still feel guilty.)

Ask yourself these questions:
- Why is it so hard for me to receive from others?
- In what areas am I particularly needy?
- What could I give someone else in return?
- Is it always necessary to reciprocate?

My Sunday school class had an enlightening discussion about this very issue last week. The topic was servanthood. The leader observed that on Jesus' last night on earth, He washed His disciples' feet. "Could we do the same thing?" she asked.

"I think I could," one woman answered. "That's not my problem, though. It's letting my feet be washed by someone else."

What is it with us? You would think they were giving out prizes for "most independent" or "most able to survive a Yukon winter alone."

Good Evangelical Christian Women appear to have a *particular* problem with receiving. The GECW is supposed to be busy at home, right? And presumably by ourselves. The GECW is supposed to do it all—from "considering a field" to "training up a child" to scraping off that gunk that plugs the gas stove burner so it won't light.

We're supposed to be the *helpers*, not the *helpless*. We worry about what other Christian women will think of us. It's difficult for us to believe that it's okay to ask for help, particularly if we grew up with a mother who seemed to do it all effortlessly—and alone. Or we're afraid we'll come across as complaining, like the feminist who whines about having to do housework. Maybe it gets back to the fear of selfishness: When was the last time you said, "I deserve this. This is my job."

I Am That I Am

Self-sufficiency is the American way, or so we think. (I just finished reading a wonderful old novel about pioneers who blazed the Oregon Trail. The story dramatically reveals how the West was won by groups, not lone rangers.) If we don't think it's the American way, at least we're sure it's the Christian way. We value privacy and autonomy above all else: One of the best-kept secrets in our churches is who is being helped by the deacons' emergency fund, and why. We're good at praying for others—we're not so great at asking for prayer ourselves.

If you're as old as I am, you'll remember a TV commercial some years ago for a headache remedy. A frowning young woman is working in the kitchen. An older woman comes in and offers to help. "Mother, please!" the younger woman snaps. "I'd rather do it myself!"

Most of us would *rather* do it ourselves. But there's a fine line between independence and pride. The Bible—which does not coddle our pride—shows another way. Throughout both the Old and New Testaments we see injunctions to care for the needy. And Paul goes into detail about the interdependence of all our body parts. The Epistles are a virtual primer on community-building within the church.

Part of building community is learning how to receive, even when there are no strings attached. It's learning that people *want* to help us, and that by allowing them to do so we are letting them share their lives—indeed, we are helping them to grow in the Christian life. Think of how you felt when you offered help to someone and were rebuffed. The GECW Syndrome—and I say this at the risk of pushing well-intended humor too far—is a malady that affects the strength-giving connective tissue of the body of Christ.

Fortunately, there are women who will have none of it.

Karen is a friend from church whose kindness I still marvel at. She does word processing at home on her computer, and knowing I was in a work crunch recently, she offered to type some pages for me. I thought she meant it in the spirit of "Let's do lunch sometime"—something nice you say to people, with no real commitment involved. So I responded with, "Well, I'm okay now—but maybe someday."

A couple of weeks later she asked me *again*. By now I wasn't just in a crunch, I was in a panic. I realized she was serious, but I still tried to talk her out of it. "Well . . . I am in kind of a bind, but I don't think you'd want to bother with it. It's . . . too hard . . . too time-consuming."

She smiled. "When do you need it?"

"In a week?" I mumbled to the floor.

Her noteworthy dimples deepened. "Just bring it over."

"What do you charge?"

"Betsey, you have no money. It'll be good experience for me. Besides, you're a writer who helps people with your words. I'm a good typist. This is something I can do for you. I'll let you pay me for something else someday."

She finished the job early and brought it by my house. The typing was flawless. Almost giddy with gratitude, I insisted that surely I could do *something* for her in return. Baby-sit. Make a casserole. Re-shingle her roof. Whatever.

"Later. After you're through this busy time."

I could not believe what I was hearing. I hardly knew how to receive this selfless gift. She moved toward her car and I hurried after her, thanking her over and over. I was almost yipping at her heels and wagging, I was that thankful. She laughed, and left quickly.

I could have insisted on paying her a token. I could have surprised her at home with chocolate cream pie from Bakers Square. Why is it so hard to be a gracious receiver? Why is it so hard to believe that Christ's love wears many faces, and some of them have dimples?

If we can overcome these barriers—false pride, embarrassment, the GECW syndrome—if we can learn to ask for help and receive it in a humble spirit, then we will have come a long way toward being gracious to ourselves and to those who might want to reach out to us.

So, Where Do You Need Help?

What are the "undecorated bedrooms" of *your* life?

Think right now about areas where you feel you're always falling behind. Things you need for the house; tasks you put off or feel unequipped to perform; activities that put you in a time crunch. To stimulate your thinking, here are a few I've come up with from my own experience and that of other women I've talked to:

- Household organization: closets, kitchen cupboards, basements and garages, paper clutter, financial records
- Mending or sewing
- Affordable child care
- Car repairs
- A better handle on managing your time
- Inexpensive children's clothes, baby furniture, strollers, car seats, playpens, cribs
- Someone to care for your pets and plants while you are out of town
- Help with yard work; access to equipment like ladders, pruning shears, snowblowers
- Expert assistance on budgeting
- Cleaning help
- Advice on smart shopping—finding the best outlet stores, resale shops, bargain basements
- Home repairs
- Support for stay-at-home moms
- Computer expertise
- Haircuts, perms
- Career counseling and networking help
- Help with spring-cleaning chores
- Access to vans and trucks for hauling things; moving assistance
- Special tutoring for children struggling with reading or math
- Help with a home business—research, typing, publicity; advice on the best deals in office furniture and equipment

If things on this list don't apply to you, they may apply

to someone else—ways you can help another person in need.

Sometimes our areas of greater need are emotional. If you think you could use one day a month just for yourself—a day to go shopping, browse bookstores, go to a park or museum, why not swap child care with a friend so she could have a similar holiday? Do you need a good laugh break? Join a couple for an evening watching a good video (there are a few).

There are times, as with my friend Karen, that we are helped and nothing is asked or expected in return. More often, though, we feel better if we can reciprocate in some way—and, when we do so, the fabric of community is woven a little deeper and stronger.

My tendency is to say, "But what can *I* do for someone else?" I feel I lack expertise in many areas. For instance, intelligent storage arrangement is not my line. (They don't call my closet the Black Hole of Futility for nothing.) I can't hang wallpaper (how many people can?) or solve computer problems. Where does that leave me on the assistance chain? Somewhere at the bottom?

Not necessarily. For example, I have a lot of stuff. I should say *we* have a lot of stuff. My husband is a saver. We always seem to have more books and blankets and suitcases, and even furniture, than we'll ever use. I'd be happy to have someone who needs it take it off my hands.

Writing is something I know. If someone needed to compose a carefully-worded letter—like complaining to a company about a product—I could do that for them. Or I could help critique an essay on a college application, or write advertising copy for a new and struggling business. These may not be pressing needs for most people most of the time—but then again, there just might be someone out there I could hook up with. (I hope they do closets.)

We *all* have skills and talents and experience. Are you a talented artist? You could give a child art lessons in exchange for something that would free up some time for you.

Maybe you could give someone a perm, write a letter of reference, plan a vegetable garden.

You could pray for someone. I'll never forget Joni Eareckson Tada's account of visiting Corrie ten Boom at her home in California. Corrie was elderly and confined to a wheelchair, but she had a powerful ministry of intercessory prayer. What gift could be more important?

There are times, too, when the best thing we can do for ourselves is to pay someone to help us—giving ourselves the gift of time. I recently hired a teenager from our church, at a modest but reasonable wage, to clean house for me alternate Saturdays. I don't mind doing it twice a month, but the weekly routine was getting to me. Emily needs the money; I need the help. It's a good exchange, and because we don't normally have much contact with teens, both my husband and I are delighted with the new friendship.

MRS. JONES, MEET THE SERVICEMASTER

The discouraging thing about housework is that it's never done. Give yourself the gift of a sparkling clean house a couple of times a year. Hire a cleaning service to do your house from top to bottom. They do carpets, windows, walls, everything. And while the service is at it, get out of the house—and have some fun.

HELP!

I need help. You need help. How do we connect?

The church is the most obvious vehicle for making it

happen. It can be an informal encounter, as when I spotted Emily lounging in the narthex and approached her about the cleaning job. Ask a friend if she knows anyone who could do whatever it is you need. Better yet, initiate a system for exchanging services, for making needs known. It could be shared in an adult Bible class or small group, where each member could mention services they feel equipped to offer. (It's amazing how little we know about the people sitting next to us in worship.) What about a regular "classified" feature in the bulletin or newsletter, or a "barter bulletin board."

Even before such an exchange can happen, however, the church must affirm itself as a community of God's people— individuals who care for one another, pray for one another, are willing to go the extra mile to meet one another's needs. There are barriers of pride and age-difference to overcome, distance, and differences in economic status. It may seem obvious that the church provide these services among it's members, but it is not as easy today as it once was. In many churches, if not most, members "commute" to worship— sometimes from distant suburbs. The church is no longer the automatic social center, with ongoing contact among members. People are busier these days, more apathetic; attendance at evening services and Wednesday-night prayer meetings attest to that.

You may be familiar with the African proverb: "It takes a whole village to raise a child." Well, it takes a whole community to help us live deeper and richer lives. Shouldn't that community spring from a body of believers?

Could you be the energetic and creative person to help initiate something in *your* church family?

Your local PTA or Christian school parents' group may also offer possibilities. Many PTAs have a "Sunshine Committee" to make meals, baby-sit, help new moms. Perhaps that could be expanded. Groups like MOPS (Mothers of Preschoolers), FEMALE (Formerly Employed Mothers at the Leading Edge), Moms in Touch, home schoolers' networks, and Christian working women's associations would also be excellent resources. If you're blessed enough to actually know your neighbors and feel comfortable with them, you might be showing Christ's love to those who may be searching for "something more."

Wherever you begin such a "resource connection," you may want to start small and expand from there. A baby-sitting co-op is a natural (just be sure you have enough people involved). I've heard of groups of men who chip in to buy expensive and infrequently-used tools and share them among themselves as needed.

Those are the key words: "share" and "need." We all have needs. We all have things to share. We don't have to stumble on alone. Learn to ask; learn to receive. It's another way to fulfill the law of Christ.

8

Give Me Some Space and Get Out of My Face

COME INTO MY STUDY with me.

You might need to put on a sweater if it's chilly, and pour yourself a mug of hot tea. It isn't winterized, but my space heater makes it cozy. On hot summer days there's always a breeze.

Don't expect anything impressive. It's not like the study of a famous author I visited a couple of times. *His* special place was a converted dining room, a large room with a chandelier and books everywhere, even on a shelf over the door. He had two big antique desks and an easy chair; comfort and space and privacy.

My study used to be our back porch. Our coats still hang in one corner. The furniture was salvaged from different parts of the house, including the basement. I have one small desk and modest filing space. Lots of books. A big braided rug on the floor. Porchy bamboo curtains at the windows.

And it's mine. (Mine . . . MINE!)

I can close the door. I have a view of the birds and the sky and the seasons—and the neighbor's garage. I have lamps that cast warm light, special photos and knickknacks and awards, indestructible plants, a radio. I do have a computer, but I'm basically low-tech: no FAX machine, no cordless phone, no "work station." But it's a place I can come to and be alone. It's *my* place. My family knows interruptions aren't real welcome when I'm back here—my husband can't leave his papers on *my* desk, and my daughter knows better than to scatter her toys on *my* floor.

A Space of Your Own

Every woman should have her own room, but many never do. Growing up, I always had to share a bedroom with my sister. I envied my friends who had their own rooms, with canopy beds and skirted dressing tables, and ballerina dolls displayed just so. I was one of four kids and our house was always noisy; I felt invaded. So I spent a lot of time sitting in the long grass of the field next to us, just hiding away by myself. My "room" was a space of prairie just big enough for one.

When I went to college I got my own room, after my roommate left in the middle of our freshman year to marry a dental student. I was glad. I had the institutional-green walls painted white, acquired a room-sized blue rug and some real furniture, and I kept the door closed—a lot. It was my sanctuary to read and think about boys and wonder about the future.

Then I got married—and lost my own room.

It was hard at first, adjusting to sleeping with another person. I would toss and turn, aware that there was another body in the queen-sized bed. I loved being married, don't get me wrong. I wasn't lonely anymore. But I needed a space for *me*. A place to retreat and think and pray and waste time.

Ladies of means have always had their own rooms. In fact, often they didn't even sleep with their husbands, addressing them formally as Mr. Smith, or whoever. They had drawing rooms in which to "receive" callers, private sewing rooms where they could dawdle the time away embroidering tea towels, or recline on a divan in genteel fragility. Governesses minded the children, and brought them to their mother at prearranged times.

Today, women have the vote, serve in Congress, and wear jeans and *Reeboks*—freedoms Scarlett O'Hara's mother would have swooned at! But many of us have lost our private space. Houses are often smaller. Extra space is likely

HARRIET'S ROOM

If I am to write, I must have a room to myself, which shall be my room. I have in my own mind pitched on Mrs. Whipple's room. We can put the stove in it. I have bought a cheap carpet for it, and there is furniture enough at home to furnish it comfortably; and I only beg in addition that you will let me change the glass door from the nursery to that room and keep my plants there, and then I shall be quite happy.
—Harriet Beecher Stowe to her husband, in 1841

to be claimed by teenagers, the third TV, and creeping clutter. Even if women work outside the home, many—nurses, teachers, telemarketers, typesetters—don't have the luxury of a private office with a door that closes. And even a private office can have a temporary feeling: You're a tenant in someone else's space. The company I worked for was forever rearranging and rebuilding, shuttling employees from office to office. I felt like out-of-season clothing being moved to another closet.

In order to be good to ourselves, to give ourselves a

chance to *stop* and think and read and rest, we need to claim a space of our own—a place we can retreat to in body and spirit.

Boundaries is the word that comes to mind.

Come No Farther

People in recovery from major life traumas understand this. Nancy LeSourd suffered an abusive childhood and writes of her experiences in *No Longer the Hero*. She says that victims of parental abuse blur the lines between themselves and their abusers, so that the child is always available to the parent and to his or her emotional or physical punishment. "We must learn to establish boundaries and set limits on the behavior of others," LeSourd says. "No, you can't do that to me." "No, that is not a proper way to talk to me."

I have a friend who is a newly single parent. I saw her at a party last night, and she was telling me what God is doing in her life as she contemplates her future, considers new career directions, discovers what the Lord has for her. We were talking about Christian women and the struggle we all have to take care of ourselves.

"I think of my mother," she said. "She had no boundaries. Anyone could interrupt her at any time, and everyone did—and we were a large family. She always ran for the phone when it rang. She 'did' for everybody. There were no limits."

If we have no set limits, then our inner selves, our very spirits, are constantly accessible, open to violation. We need to have a firm *yes* and a firm *no* (as Scripture itself teaches). "Yes, I can help." "No, I will not answer the phone now." "You cannot treat me this way." "I will not assume your pain or your need; I am not you."

This is especially hard for mothers. When my daughter scrapes her knee, I can almost feel the sting. I sometimes wish I could be at school with her, protecting her from boys on the playground who kick her snow fort over. If she needs me, I don't want to turn away from her.

But it is not harmful for my child to learn early in life that I sometimes need time alone. Time to just relax and reflect. Time with myself.

When inner boundaries are threatened, the abused child looks for a place to hide and, finding none, often builds a wall around his or her emotions, thus growing into an adult who cannot trust anyone. We all—even the emotionally healthy—need hiding places where our souls can find refuge.

It's instructive how often the Psalms use this language— God as our *refuge*, God as our *hiding place*, God as our *fortress*. Our first need is to "hide" in the Lord, the ultimate safe place, drawing strength through prayer and meditation and time in His Word. God is, truly, a space all our own.

We also need to break the habit of constant, no exceptions, availability.

Often, someone else can answer the phone. Our children can learn to wait when they want something *now*. We can learn to think twice when someone asks for our help. (Usually someone else can provide the same help.) Look for alternatives to being in constant demand.

A while ago a friend asked me if I could take a meal to a family whose child is in the hospital with cancer. I had signed up at the church to help in this way, but that particular night wasn't convenient because I was going out of town on business the next day. Still, I hesitated, not wanting to let someone down. *I could whip up something . . .*

Then I decided I just couldn't do it. "No," I said apologetically, "I can't do it this time." Then I blurted, "I can't believe it. I actually said no to something."

My friend laughed and hugged me. "Relax. I still like you," she said.

"Thanks, I needed that."

Often, saying yes to everything is just a matter of practice: If you always say yes it becomes an ingrained habit. You don't even think about it. I'm not saying the reverse has to be true, where you say no to everything. But stop and think. It's okay to say no when you are overloaded. (And no explanation is necessary.) It is interesting to note that if you say no a few times you aren't asked as often either.

Whither Goest Thou?

But *where* do we go for time alone?

Sometimes we flee to the bathroom and take a long shower. Or we jump into our car and drive somewhere, just to be alone; we play tapes, or listen to the radio, and shut out the world (as much as that is possible with tons of metal hurtling around you at breakneck speeds.)

Who hasn't folded laundry, typed letters, or nursed an infant and let their mind drift off—tiny moments, stolen moments, moments alone.

It's not enough, though. If I could have a perfect life, I would have two hideaways in addition to my study—because, although it is mine, it is also a place that screams *work*.

In fine weather I would repair to a summer house, like one of those screened outbuildings Victorian estates boast. The little place would be furnished in white wicker with flowery chintz cushions. There would be a glider heaped with pillows, a stack of books and magazines next to it. There would be a round table set with a crystal pitcher of lemonade and a heaping dish of raspberries and cream. I would read all the books that I buy but never get around to enjoying. No one would know where I was.

My cold-weather retreat would be a garret apartment at the top of a four-story Georgian townhouse as seen in Boston's Beacon Hill, or Paris. The place would have dormer windows overlooking an ever-changing cityscape. There would be a spectacular view of a harbor or river. I would curl up on a window seat, warmed by a Franklin stove, and write books longhand, the way Louisa May Alcott and Emily Dickenson did. If I got sleepy I could nap on a high bed built into an alcove in the wall. The silent butler would deliver a tray of steaming bouillabaisse and crusty bread for my lunch. (Notice the prominence of food in these pictures . . .)

Couldn't you live with that? Of course you could!

But until I figure out a way to write a best-seller on the level of *Where's Waldo?* I guess I'll have to live with my view of the neighbor's garage, and with whatever other private nook I can carve out for myself.

Me-Places

Having a physical space we can claim as our own helps define boundaries. So often at the disposal of others, we women need something we can call our own. Even if it's a corner, or a chair.

There's a wonderful children's book called *A Chair for My Mother.* A girl of eight or nine tells the story of how a fire destroyed her family's belongings, and they were forced to rely on the kindness of relatives for furniture. The only chairs they had were straight-back kitchen chairs. The child's mother worked as a waitress, and at night she would come home to their small apartment and collapse in a kitchen chair. Together they hatched the idea of saving the mother's restaurant tips in a jar: When they had enough change they would go to the bank and exchange it for dollars. Then they would buy a nice, comfy armchair. It took a long time, but one day they counted the coins and it was enough. They chose a beautiful rose-patterned easy chair. The tired mom relaxed in it every evening, and the little girl would curl up in her lap.

If you don't have a chair of your own, a chair that fits you, I suggest you find one. It could be a Laura Ashley-print wingback with matching hassock, or an old canvas slingback, as long as it is comfortable for you, and everyone in the family knows it's yours (including family pets). If possible, set a small table with a lamp next to it, and keep a basket nearby for magazines, books, Bible, sewing, whatever. Preferably, keep your chair away from the TV and the phone. You may want it in your bedroom, a place generally private, at least during the day (you'll have to train your husband not to toss his clothes on it.)

You can also carve out spaces alone throughout the day. When I am regulating my life the way I prefer, I am up early and sit at our breakfast-nook kitchen table before anyone else is around. I love this table. It's oak, I think, big and sturdy—my husband stained it blue and varnished it. I refuse to allow it to collect clutter. When I get up in the morning, it is ready for me, clear and shiny. The coffeemaker is set to brew at six. I sit in the corner chair and write, or read my Bible. Sometimes I enjoy just sitting and watching the dawn. To keep the table that special place at sunrise, I avoid sitting there to do kitchen chores later in the day.

Some kitchens have an alcove with a desk. These are great for a woman's restful retreat. It's also practical for writing letters, making lists, keeping the calendar updated. If you have one, make it your own. Don't let anyone else sit there!

If your car is your only haven away from it all, keep it washed and waxed, and clear of refuse inside. Cluttered or dirty environments are an underrated stressor. Here are a few tips:

- Insist that everyone you cart around retrieve their stuff from the car.
- Reserve some times when you aren't driving anyone except you.
- Use a car freshener that mimics a new-car smell, or maybe you prefer one that smells like Mom's apple pie.
- Avoid cellular phones, unless you absolutely require one for your business.
- Keep an attractive non-spill mug on the dash.

- Listen to books-on-tape, or maybe just your favorite music.
- Find a scenic route if you commute to work by car (what must it do to the senses and the soul to look at strip malls and Jiffy Lube stations day after day?)

If you have any say at all about your office space at your place of work, by all means speak up. A few years ago I was stuck in a dark, windowless cubicle by the coffee station and the coat rack. I hated it. I'm sure it affected my attitude about coming to work every day. (I would have taken a new office over a raise.) Then I heard a rumor that a co-worker was going to vacate a corner office with a big window. I immediately went to my supervisor's boss: "I've heard Nancy's moving to the first floor," I said. "If she does, I'd like to put in a bid for her office." He said he would speak to the appropriate people.

A few weeks later he called me in. "The office is yours," he said. "We can't give you the big raise you deserve this year, but we hope this move will show how much we value you and your work."

I realize such a move isn't always possible, especially in a large organization, where office allocation and even the wall decor is determined at corporate headquarters. But if you have a good relationship with your superiors, and have proven your worth as an employee, give it a try. If they're reasonable and care about their personnel, they can't fire you for asking. I stayed in that office-with-a-view for more than five years, happily looking out at incoming storms, reddening leaves, flying finches, and the pink Mary Kay semi that passed regularly. (And I did get a lot of work done; probably more.) I've read that if your senses are kept busy with pleasant things to look at and listen to, creativity is released.

Caution: Do not make your office look like something out of a Martha Stewart style book. It will not likely be understood by your employers.

Squatters' Rights

Then there are those spaces that don't necessarily belong to you, but they *become* yours by virtue of frequent use, and they do function as a retreat and an escape. You may need to get out of the house and away from work to find a place of your own without distraction. A bench at a safe park could serve this purpose in good weather. (Remember, we are not worrying about what people think.) You could go continental and sit drinking exotic coffee at a local restaurant, especially during off hours when the space isn't at a premium. (Bring a book, write a letter, or work in your journal.)

If you need a quiet place for regular prayer, your pastor might be happy to let you use a room in the church. Public libraries are at once restful and stimulating. They're clean and neat, don't cost anything, and it's fun to disappear into the stacks, looking at biographies or travel books or oversized volumes of art or whatever interests you. The point is to have a place you return to often, something of your own.

Regularity is another key.

There's a lot about the Christian life that's unexpected, that has to do with grace and surprise, serendipity. But there's also a lot that has to do with order and repetition and disciplined habit, even for us free-church types. Regular prayer. Observance of the Lord's Day. Systematic Bible reading. Weekly worship. Planned giving to God's work. Most of us at least *try* to practice these disciplines with some degree of regularity. We wouldn't think of saying, "Oh gee, I'm free this Sunday—guess I'll go to church!"

But do we give ourselves, our space, our time the same attention? Do we view our time alone as a spiritual necessity? In most cases, probably not.

I'm not going to add to your Montana-sized load of guilt by telling you that you must take an hour for yourself, every day, at six in the morning! (Don't you do that to yourself, either.) Don't let what should be a delight become another burden, another legalism. I *do* encourage you to think in terms of taking a little time every day, or several longer periods during the week, to spend time alone, doing whatever rests you and revitalizes you best. Find the pattern that fits your lifestyle. Make it a time you look forward to, that you enjoy. If you get bored with it, change the time, change the place, change the activity. You're too good to be content with the same humdrum, day in and day out.

To avoid this, be sure that your special time is not spent at doing anything that smells or looks like "chores." You may wish to do absolutely nothing. Daydream, anticipate a pleasant event. Write poetry that will never be published (not every effort has to bring "results"). Think about Jesus' love for you and feel *washed* in that love. It can be a productive time, spiritually or emotionally, or just be a time to unwind, rest, rejuvenate. (Don't worry about anyone else. They will survive!)

When I allow myself this time and this space, I can always feel how much I needed it. I'm like a drought-stricken field responding to rain, like a love-deprived child responding to a good hug. Then I wonder, *What have I denied myself? How did my soul become so needy?* So needy, sometimes, that anything I do to nurture it is instantly appreciated—and applauded by God, I believe.

Everyone needs a *place*—both a physical setting and an emotional retreat. A place to *be*, to grow—like a tree needs space and time to sink its roots deep. Because women so often share their time and space with others, they especially need an island, an oasis all their own.

So, do yourself a favor, friend. Give yourself a room, a chair, time for your soul. And if you're really desperate, you could use my study. Just remember to turn on the heater.

9

How Do You Find the Time to Spend With God?

HOW'S YOUR DEVOTIONAL LIFE these days? More haphazard than you'd like? Do you have trouble finding time to spend with God? Do you sometimes feel stale and dissatisfied, and think the problem *must* be you?

Sometimes I feel like running away from my quiet time with God, rather than rushing toward it. Instead of seeing it as the wellspring of spiritual refreshment it is meant to be, it becomes one more obligation. Ah, there it is then: more work; more duty; the kiss of death.

Lots of women struggle with this one. I would like to tell you that I'm up before cockcrow every morning, poring over the *Thompson Chain-Reference Bible*, clutching a prayer list as long as a roll of paper towels. I would like to say that my devotional times are always spiritually refreshing, that my mind never wanders, that I always gain some life-altering insight. The only problem is that it would not be true.

The secret of spiritual refreshment is to live with God at the center of our lives. Actively. Joyfully. Regularly. When we do that, everything else tends to fall into place.

Okay, so that's the goal. How do we refresh a worn-out

attitude toward our personal spiritual lives? What about the care and feeding of our souls?

MAKE YOURSELF AT HOME

I think distractions in prayer come because we have allowed ourselves to wander too far from the things that matter most. We slip into an easily interrupted, easily distracted frame of mind. We need to live "at home." "In him we live and move and have our being" (Acts 17:28). This means, simply, God is our home.

Home of my heart, lest I forget
    My redemption's cost to Thee,
Let my earliest thought be set
    Upon Thy Calvary.

These words, which center my attention on what matters most, speak of something that I cannot drop out of my day without great loss to me.

—Amy Carmichael, You Are My Hiding Place

Somehow we've gotten the idea that "time with God" has to follow a certain pattern to be truly spiritual. We're supposed to use a "daily reading plan," refer to a prayer list, regularly updated. (This may sound irreverent, but does anyone besides me ever feel guilty about dropping someone from a prayer list? Or do most people just keep adding names?) And we're supposed to do this at the same time each day—every day. Gee, sounds like work to me.

Next thing you know we're going to have to punch-in for our quiet time.

Some years ago, J. B. Phillips wrote a book called *Your God Is Too Small*. To that I might add, "Our idea of the devotional life is too small."

I don't dismiss the role of *discipline* and *commitment* in the Christian life. But too often there's an element of *set-your-jaw* grimness in our approach to a devotional time. I don't believe God wants us to draw near to Him with resignation, the way we approach filling out our tax return.

He does, however, want us to draw near to Him. How can we put God first when there's little quiet and less time in our lives? How can we renew a humdrum devotional life?

Brother Lawrence Revisited

Earlier I referred to Brother Lawrence's idea of "practicing the presence"—committing even the most mundane tasks to the Lord. We can place so much emphasis on a separate devotional time that we can forget that *everything* we do and think and say should in some way be consecrated to God. Time with God, then, is less a task to be performed than an awareness to be lived out.

Let's start with gratitude. Consider your immediate environment as you're reading this. What is the weather like? Where are you sitting? (In that special chair, I hope.) Who made the weather? Who provided the roof that shelters you from the weather? Who gave you the children whose pictures sit on your dresser, the husband whose smile hasn't changed since that wedding portrait was taken? Who led you to the church whose newsletter waits in your things-to-read basket?

As I write this, it is early winter ... midmorning ... midweek. Just an ordinary work day. But I look out the window and notice the pattern of the bare trees against the ice-blue sky. I watch a squirrel scaling the summit of an elm and wonder how she stays warm. Amanda's tire swing will not be in use today. I hear a chickadee peeping and am grateful for the life he brings to this bleak landscape. I thank God for all these things.

I also thank God for quiet, homely indoor things: something warm to drink, the sweater I'm wearing (even though I'm forever whining about my clothes, or shortage thereof), the *whoosh* of the furnace (even though I'm always complaining about our gas bill), the picture my daughter drew in Sunday school . . . Ordinary things, easily overlooked. But God is in them as surely as He is in the grandeur of sky and season.

THE FINAL RESTING PLACE OF PRAYER

Gratitude is not a prayer that comes easy for me. For difficulties resolved, salvation realized, prayers answered, yes. But for my life— its responsibilities, demands, hardships, hopes—I have not always been grateful. In fact, from early on, even after I became a Christian, I have resented having to live life with so many burdens. But by the mercies of Christ's grace I have turned a corner. That, too, is a gift.

Spiritual leaders will tell you that gratefulness is the final resting place of prayer. It is the basic recognition that one's very life is not earned or learned, a bribe or a reward, but a free gift. Gratefulness is the vulnerable, emotional rise of joy in appreciation of that gift. And before long other appreciations connect to it! In that gratitude is some of the abundance of life our Lord promised.

—Mary C. Miller

I'm grateful for my work and the passion I bring to it. I'm equally thankful I'm starting to learn when to give myself respites from that work. I thank God for books, for eloquent Christian authors, for pastors, for ideas. For friends, for the gift of laughter, for the gift of healing tears. First and last, for my salvation.

As we consciously praise and thank the Lord for everything He has done for us—or, even more deeply, praise Him because He is God and therefore worthy of our worship—we are spending time with Him. We can do this throughout our day. Say a prayer out loud, think it or just feel it. This sense of gratitude is an ongoing way to be with God, to offer our "sacrifice of praise" up to Him.

Here's something I came across the other day that expresses inward praise as well as anything I've read for a long time. It's a declaration of St. Augustine, from his *Confessions*: "And the happy life is this: To rejoice *in* you. To rejoice *for* you. To rejoice *because* of you. I say it again: Life is joy in you, who are the Truth, O my God, the light of my soul, the health of my body!"

Where the Bible Leather Meets the Road

Here's something else that happens to me—and maybe to you too.

I'm having my quiet time, having managed to carve out fifteen spare minutes between mountains of laundry. I've opened a book to read—an approved devotional aid or collection of lofty thoughts. I sit and read the first page . . . And then I read the first page again. And then my mind starts wandering, and a little voice inside whispers, *This is really boring and hard to follow.*

Of course I feel guilty and sort of shallow for thinking that. Christians are supposed to steep themselves in the great literature of spiritual giants from times past (aren't they?) The problem is, much of the language is archaic for me, a modern reader, and the writing can be dry and dense.

Those cute little *thought-a-day* books, on the other hand, sometimes don't provide enough spiritual nourishment. It's like eating one M & M—hardly enough. You're left feeling like you should have tasted something, but . . .

What else—besides, of course, Scripture—is there?

Here again we run into the walls of the devotional box. Where did we get the cloistered idea that "This is devotional literature, and this is not?" God wants us to draw near to Him, and we can open a number of doors to catch a glimpse.

For instance, I enjoy some fiction. I enjoy personal-experience stories. I enjoy books and articles that I can apply to my life. I think most women do. Who said we can't use these as devotional aids? Here are a few examples of such literature:

- Spiritual autobiographies, such as C. S. Lewis' *Surprised by Joy*, or a modern translation of St. Augustine's *Confessions*
- Inspiring stories of pioneer missionaries
- Fiction with spiritual themes, including the classics by novelists like Dostoyevsky
- Books that deal with some challenge of the Christian life, such as Philip Yancey's *Disappointment With God*
- Quality children's literature
- Articles in Christian magazines

Maybe you're already enjoying one or more of the above. To approach your reading from a more "devotional" standpoint, I suggest you read *prayerfully*, asking the Holy Spirit to open your eyes and heart to whatever insight He may choose to reveal. You may want to keep a highlighter in hand, underlining certain passages. Or you may simply want to be inspired with a sense of God's presence. However you choose to read, know that this, too, can be time with God.

Turn On the Tunes

Music also has the power to renew our souls. We often play Christian tapes at our house—an admittedly eclectic assortment, ranging from the newer praise instrumentals, to George Beverly Shea, to Phil Keaggy. Sometimes—let us be charitable but honest—even Christian music, especially the contemporary variety, can become tiresome and over-familiar. Too many multi-tracked synthesizers or something. Then the soul longs for something more, something majestic and soaring and . . . I don't know . . . *large* is a word that comes to mind.

If you mostly listen to Christian radio, try switching to National Public Radio or a classical station in your area. Do chores as you listen, or sit and pay close attention. Sooner or later you'll probably hear a piece that particularly moves you. The composer may not be "Christian" by our evangelical definition, but consider this: Handel began his *Messiah* as a purely commissioned work, yet who has sat through a performance of *The Messiah* and failed to hear in the music the thunder of God?

Music stores often sell classical tapes and CDs at bargain prices. Go buy a few. Get to know various composers and their works. Familiarize yourself with different periods of music. I find Gregorian chants particularly restful. I have no idea *what* they're chanting, but I love to listen and feel connected to an ancient time when all things—from music to planting to art to conquest—were done under the over-arch of Faith.

One key to enjoying devotional music and its lyrics is *focus*. My pastor has a habit of quoting from hymns in his sermons. When he does this, I home in on what I think the writer intended, and I gain a fresh appreciation for the meaning of the hymns. When we sing in church we're often concentrating so hard on following the tune that we miss the significance of the text; or, if the hymn is familiar, we miss the meaning because we've heard it so much. Try this sometime: *Read a hymnal or songbook.* Say the words aloud or just reflect on them. Find a new hymn or rediscover a classic. Some of the texts will resound in your soul.

For example, what could be more majestic than Isaac

Watts' "Before the hills in order stood/Or earth received her frame/From everlasting Thou art God/To endless years, the same"?

Why isn't anyone writing like that anymore?

If you can't seem to find the time, or the time you spend in devotions is dry, maybe you need a fellow believer to help you. There's nothing wrong with admitting, "I can't do this alone."

You might want to seek your pastor's advice. He'll be delighted that you're taking your Christian life seriously, and he may have some books to pass on or helpful insights to share. I am increasingly convinced it is important to seek out persons whom we feel are further along in their spiritual journey than we are, to figuratively sit at their feet and learn from them. There's something wonderfully humbling about being in the presence of a truly godly man or woman and thinking, *This person is wiser than I am.* Some Christians go so far as to find a "spiritual director," someone they meet with on a regular basis who helps guide their spiritual life.

Prayer partnerships can be mutually enriching. When you covenant with another person to meet regularly for prayer, you make yourself accountable to that individual, and she to you.

Once More, Please, From the Heart

What do you pray about? I lose the passionate fire of prayer when my real gut-level concern for something or someone wanes. Too often I try to pray out of a sense of guilt or duty—and guess what happens. Do you think you always have to have a prayer list? Do you really *care* about all the concerns on that list?

Many times prayer requests are along these lines: "My neighbor's cousin's daughter's fifth child has had eczema for six weeks." And I'm supposed to get "fervent"? On the other hand, "My husband is scared he's going to be laid off," or "I'm lonely," or "We're broke" sends me to my knees.

And then there are admonitions from Paul, like "Pray without ceasing." Boy, did *that* used to undo me. Okay, we *should* pray about everything and do it without ceasing. But here you are, coming to your chair, desperate for some solace. Maybe *you're* the one who's lonely or broke, or maybe it's just been a bad week and you feel the need to pull your scattered self back together. Sometimes we face our prayer list with guilt *and* coldness—when the first priority might be to take ourselves, the pieces of our scattered lives, one by one, and turn them over to God. You could even say it *out loud*: "Lord, I'm so worried about _____. I know you're in control. I trust you. Here's my burden. I put it in your hands."

David Mains, in his book *Eight Survival Skills for Changing Times*, takes the idea a step further, suggesting we need to bring *one* immediate concern before God in our prayers. He notes that Jesus said in Matthew 6, "Therefore do not worry about tomorrow, for tomorrow will worry about itself. Each day has enough trouble of its own."

"To pray too far into the future almost discourages faith," Mains says. "It's like saying, 'I assume little is going to change for the good in the next month, Lord.' "

I know I've done that to God—backed up the truck and unloaded a warehouseful of worries. Sure, God can deal with them—*but can we?* Sometimes it helps our own focus to zero-in on the most immediate need: "I have a meeting with my boss tomorrow." "My child is waking up a lot at night." "I'm worried about my dad; he hasn't seemed well lately." You might even want to write it down. Putting a concern on paper—*naming* the worry—somehow makes it seem more concrete and therefore more manageable. Prayer lists are fine—if they help you to keep certain people and needs in mind. Intercessory prayer can literally make miracles happen.

But let's not forget that we will grow cold to prayer if we lose the heart-connection that is the soul of prayer. Make sure you can pray through your list with authenticity, really caring about the concerns you're bringing to the Lord and not just reciting names and places and needs.

Sometimes God will bring certain people to mind while I am praying: Billy Graham, being treated for Parkinson's disease; Christian teachers in our local public schools; friends who recently adopted a baby; unknown women facing crisis pregnancies. Then I know His Spirit is moving through the world, whispering His concerns to my heart, sharing them, as it were, with me. *This is very refreshing, to know that God trusts me with these needs.*

Try *Not* Talking at All in Prayer

There are also times when we come before God in silence—without words or petitions, basking in His presence, seeking the rest He brings.

A church we attended held a prayer vigil on a Saturday. People came to the church's small chapel and prayed for as long as they wished—or just sat quietly before the Lord. I went in and sat for a while. Then I knelt (I felt driven to my knees), not because I had any great petition to offer, but because I was overwhelmed by His presence. I was oblivious to anything but my smallness and God's divine greatness. I didn't think anything, just *sensed*. It was more than enough. It was healing.

There are times when our overloaded nervous system needs a chance to knit itself back together. We live in such a noisy, hyped-up world. Even our worship services sometimes barrage us: Someone's always talking, singing, trying to motivate us. Very rarely are we *left alone* to experience complete quiet—a sense of awe. It is often in that silence that we can hear God the most clearly. Who is training us to handle silence?

BEYOND THE SMELLS AND BELLS

It's easy to get put off by the outward trappings of another brand of Christianity, but often that's because we haven't explored other traditions. Becoming acquainted with other forms of worship can give our own spiritual life a boost, both as we discover the varied riches of God's church, and are moved to reaffirm our own traditions.

If you're from a "low-church" background, ask a Catholic or Orthodox friend if you could attend a mass with him/her, or a Holy Week observance. If you're more accustomed to solemnly liturgical worship, visit a Pentecostal congregation. If you're white, ask a black friend if you could join her for worship on Sunday. (If you visit a Mennonite church, make sure there's a potluck afterward!)

"Where is the house you will build for me? Where will my resting place be?" God asks in Isaiah 66:1. When I saw that passage it hit me with a jolt, like an electric shock.

Am I building my house for the Lord?

It's still under construction, and the decor may not be flawless . . . but I'm trying.

And that, I think, is what God wants. Not necessarily a *by-the-book* "devotional time." Habit without heart. He wants to live in our houses of the soul, yours and mine.

Invite Him in. Regularly. Can you sense Him, waiting for you?

10

Sometimes I Feel Like Running Away From My Demanding Self

WHAT WOULD BE THE GREATEST GIFT someone could give you? Something that would last, make your life easier, make you more content.

If someone were to ask me what I wanted most—if I could have anything in the world, I think it would be this: the gift of accepting myself just as I am, just as God made me. And to concentrate on pleasing Him above all, regardless of what anyone else may think.

Doughnuts and Pleasing God

We were gathered in the sanctuary on Sunday to view a Larry Burkett video. He may be a fine brother in Christ with much valuable information to say about finances, but Larry Burkett isn't . . . fun. So we had doughnuts. It was amusing to watch seventy-five men and women descend on the goodies like locusts on a Kansas wheat field. I was disciplined, of course; I only took two small doughnut holes. After all, what would people think if I snarfed down one of those big glazed jobs? Could I bear the guilt of causing a weaker sister to stumble? Maybe I could sneak one . . .

Then there was a second, even more interesting round of doughnuts. Heads swerved from the video screen as Deacon Tom hefted another box onto the table. Only the men went for seconds, that is, except for my friend, Cathy. We talked about this later. I can kid Cathy about these things. Or, maybe I should say, Cathy can *accept* being kidded. Face it, a lot of us can't.

"Oh, I knew I was the only woman up there," Cathy said. "But now that I'm past forty, I figure I'll just live in this big body and not worry about it."

Cathy does not have a "big body." She, like every woman in North America, except maybe Cindy Crawford, would like to lose a few pounds. This body image thing has gotten out of hand. My point is that Cathy wanted a second doughnut, and she was not about to let what people *might* think stand in her way.

Then I asked Cathy where her husband, John, was. "Home with a bad cold. The kids wanted to stay home with him, so I said 'Why not?' He never gets to spend time with them. When I left they were going to act out a Bible story— with John as a dead king, so he wouldn't have to move from the couch."

We agreed it was probably more important for John, who works all day Saturdays, to be with his children on an occasional Sunday morning than to be in church. It is so easy for church attendance to become a demand instead of a joy. Again, Cathy was confident and serene in her decision. She was not worried about what people thought.

I admire my friend's ability to distance herself from false pressures—her ability to achieve self-acceptance. I wish I could be more like her; less concerned with people's opinions, more secure in my own. There's something convoluted about envying someone because she doesn't envy others. Earth to Elizabeth: *Is there a lesson here?*

Here's the lesson, I believe: Cathy has stopped running away from herself. She is running *toward* freedom—freedom in honest self-acceptance and self-assessment. Freedom in God's love.

118

DOES GOD HAND OUT REPORT CARDS?

Many (dare I say, most?) Christians live their lives as though they are going to be graded once a year by a God who stands there frowning, with his hands stuck in the pockets of his robe. (I don't know why, but probably most people usually think of God with a robe on, never in sweats or cutoffs or a swimsuit. . . . He's always wearing a beard and this white robe.) Glaring, He says, "Well, Johnson that gets a C-." And, "Dorothy, you ought to be ashamed!" And, "Smith? Not bad. Could've been better, though." What heretical imaginations we have!

Why do we think like that? Who is responsible for such horror-images of the Almighty? Where did we pick up the idea that God is mad or irritated? Knowing that all of God's wrath was poured out on His son at His death on the cross, how can we think like that? As a matter of fact, the reason He brought Jesus back from the grave is that He was satisfied with His Son. Ponder this: If the Father is satisfied with His Son's full payment for sin, and we are in His Son, by grace through faith, then He is satisfied with you and me. How long must we Christians live before we finally believe that?

—Charles R. Swindoll

What Are We Really Running Away From?

I wonder if the "sometimes I feel like running away from home" impulse that seizes us occasionally is, in truth, an impulse to run away from our *selves*, or at least our own demanding *view* of ourselves. We are trying to tune out that critical, self-destructive voice inside us, much like those who suffer from tinnitus (ringing in the ears) have music playing so they can escape the constant, maddening drone.

We feel like we want to borrow someone else's life for a while. Or suddenly be a new and improved version of what God has made us (not *too* improved, though; Christians are supposed to be humble, right?)

As a Christian, do you feel caught in a maddening crush—between the self you *are* and the self you think you *ought* to be?

"Do not think of yourself more highly than you ought," counsels Paul in Romans 12:3. We always remember that part. But he goes on: ". . . but rather think of yourself with sober judgment, in accordance with the measure of faith God has given you."

With sober judgment. As we really are, *right now*? Gifts, warts, and all? That's right. You accept yourself and move on—"with the measure of faith God has given you."

It's hard to see yourself as you are. It's a little like knowing what we really look like. When I look in my bathroom mirror, by the soft flattering light, I pose and admire my high cheekbones. I avoid looking at my bad side, the side where my nose looks lumpy. (As you can see, I have studied this in detail.)

On the other hand, when I have my picture taken I put on a frozen, self-conscious expression just as the flash goes off. In every photo I look pasty-faced and glassy-eyed. The light is too harsh.

Does anyone really know what they look like? (Surely you've had the disconcerting experience of catching a glimpse of yourself as you pass a store window. Who *is* that hunched woman with the unflattering skirt length?)

Most of us have an unclear view of ourselves. We either avoid the light of truth, or we overexpose ourselves so that every hideous flaw becomes monstrous. Before we can find true freedom and rest as children of God, we need to give ourselves the gift of balanced *self-acceptance.*

Think for a moment. If you are married, think about how you love your husband *despite* his shortcomings. (This is assuming, I know.) You know he's not perfect, but you don't expect perfection in him. You can feel the same way about your children, your parents, your friends. You aren't always comparing them against some ideal. You celebrate their gifts and overlook their flaws. But do you give yourself the same break?

HOW CAN YOU FORGET YOURSELF IF YOU DON'T KNOW WHO YOU ARE?

My grandmother always took pride in her appearance. She was called the "best-dressed lady in church." For a poor widow she was very elegant, because she had a sense of creativity, especially when it came to decorating her hats and remaking her dresses. She was a lady in the best sense of the word, excelled in the art of self-acceptance. She had learned the secret of Simone de Beauvoir's words: "It is the task of every woman to forget herself, but how can she do that if she doesn't know who she is? Some women never learn to know who they are, and that's why they have so little to give others." My grandmother knew who she was, and this made her one who could speak wisely and with authority.

—Ingrid Trobisch

This running away from ourselves follows a tortuous course. Does any of the below apply to you?

- You feel you often fail to live up to your own standards for yourself . . .

- . . . An inner voice regularly reminds you of that fact.
- You feel you often fail to live up to the standards of others.
- You think celebrating the gifts God has given you shows pride on your part.
- You worry about what others think.
- You look toward some bright day when everything in your life will be perfect.

Something I read recently by Paul Tournier has stayed with me. Many people, he writes, struggle with "a sort of prejudice" against themselves. It's not exactly low self-esteem—more the keen awareness of how great the gap is between their expectations and their perceived inadequate reality. The more deeply we want to serve Christ, the more discouraged we become about our failings in that area. The more we long to use the gifts God has given us, the more we feel like we squander those gifts. The more we thirst to be a better friend, spouse, parent, the more we realize we never measure up in those roles. And the odd thing is, we feel as though everyone else *does* measure up. Ironically, says Tournier, the more gifted and sensitive the individual, the more intensely she feels herself to be a grown-up underachiever.

Whence comes this pain? Tournier doesn't speculate, but I have one idea, and it comes from my childhood. I was a strange student—off-the-charts talented in some areas and bafflingly inept in others. I didn't like to work hard at things I wasn't good at. (I still don't.) So my grades, especially when I hit adolescence, were as up and down as an abnormal electrocardiogram. When I was a sophomore in high school I had the vocabulary of a college senior, and I was flunking freshman algebra! Here is what I kept hearing: "You're so bright. If only you could do better. If only you could work up to your capabilities. If you would just *try*."

If only you could do better . . . awwk . . . If only you could do better—Parrot that to yourself enough and you're going to believe it. I'm convinced that those early messages to a sensitive kid encoded themselves in my brain so that now, no matter what the accomplishment, I find it hard to pat myself on the back. Instead, I'm more likely to give myself a kick in the pants and say, "It isn't good enough."

An example: I just received the galleys on a book for which I had an almost impossible deadline. I was pleased with the result. It's a good book. But even as I looked through the manuscript, I was thinking, *You were late on this. You have another project to do. You're running behind on that. How are you going to finish everything? Why are you such a procrastinator, anyway?*

So I forced myself to celebrate. I took the manuscript to a writers' group I'm involved in, waved it at them and said, "*Look!* I did this, and it's good! Hooray for me!"

Dumb, I know, but it was a breakthrough—to simply seize the moment, to acknowledge that life is fine and there are things I do rather well, thanks be to God. Somehow I managed, this time, not to poison the moment by thinking, *Yes, but look at the piles in my office.*

Say What?

There goes that little voice again! Psychologists use the term "self-talk" to describe one way we send ourselves messages. Self-talk can be positive (I *can* do it), or negative (I'll never make it). All of us who struggle with low self-esteem are bedeviled—(interesting term there) by that voice.

What do you most often tell yourself *about* yourself?

Let's say you get up in the morning and the house is a mess. Crumbs on the carpet, couch cushions in disarray, dishes piled in the sink. Do you think, *What a wreck this place is! Why can't I get on top of the housework?* Or do you think, *Isn't it nice that the junior high group had so much fun here last night?*

Do you look in the mirror and automatically go, *Arrgghh?* Or do you think, *Hmmm, I got a good haircut this time.* (Or do you avoid mirrors whenever possible?)

Do you tell yourself, *I'll never be as successful as my sister?* Or have you learned to accept the fact that you and she are different people with different gifts *and* faults, and you really wouldn't want her life anyway?

Christian cognitive therapy teaches people to recognize their unhealthy thinking processes, and to reorient their thinking accordingly. Whether your negative self-talk comes from your childhood, or wrong ideas about being a good Christian, or something else, *it is possible to reorient your thinking.* Maybe not easy—because sometimes it's very deeply rooted—but possible.

Rather than try to switch overnight to all positive self-talk, try this: Every day, speak the positive truth to yourself. If you and your child are having a happy time together, for example, tell yourself, *You know, I'm not doing a bad job as a mom.* If you successfully resisted temptation at lunch and ordered the salad (dressing on the side) instead of what you *really* wanted, say to yourself, *Good for me! I'm learning to eat right.*

Although this may feel forced at first, eventually it will become more of a habit, and good habits crowd out the bad. You can learn to engage in *realistic* self-talk, which brings us back to Paul's "sober judgment." If I'm behind on a book I can say to myself, *Yes, I'm behind—but I'll make it. Besides, the editor really liked the last batch of chapters I sent him.* I can escape the trap of making sweeping condemnations about myself—and so can you.

Another thing I do is to keep a collection of "warm fuzzies" I've received—nice notes, compliments (yes, sometimes I write them down), cards. From time to time, it helps to take them out and reread some of them and remind myself that people *do* care.

Just maybe there's a word from God in there. A bit of light, shed by other people who love you, that says something about you and who you are becoming in Christ.

As we begin to see ourselves with clearer vision, other perspectives, we can affirm our strengths and build on them. We can stop worrying about our weaknesses, or trying to be someone we're *not*.

Be Who You Are—With All Your Might

My daughter's school has an active PTA, but don't count me in. School politics, endless night meetings, discussion of school board decisions bore me. It's not my thing. I appreciate the work of those parents who *are* involved. But I don't feel guilty about opting out.

Paul, himself, is an example of a person who had a wise self-assessment. He was a gifted church-planter, speaker, and missionary who left the nuts-and-bolts work of maintaining the ministry to others. He was gifted in encouragement and exhortation, but I suspect he would not have been happy staying in one place and becoming, in effect, a denominational bureaucrat. He could say, candidly, "I wish all could be as I am." He could also talk about his affliction. Paul knew his strengths and weaknesses, and didn't have to take an aptitude test to find out what they were.

Of course Paul did not have a spouse and kids to contend with. But his "children" were the baby Christians scattered all over the Mediterranean world. In our own marriages and parenting, we can find our strengths and build on them, and not spin our wheels trying to live up to some ideal that denies our basic personality—whether that standard is set by ourselves or by others.

A lot of marriage-enrichment advice, for example, counsels couples to sit down and talk about goals for their marriage, to take tests together and compare the results—*Give your marriage a checkup. How well do you know your spouse? What's your five-year plan?* I hate stuff like that. But you may enjoy it, and it may be really helpful to you. Just don't force yourself into the mold if it is not for you.

YELLOW SHOES AND OTHER WAYS TO GIVE YOURSELF A LIFT

All of us spend a lot of time worrying about how we look. Some of us may think we need a full body transplant to feel better about ourselves. But sometimes just a little change can give us a big boost.

For example: Change your makeup. Many of us are quick to update our hairstyles or clothing, but not our makeup. Even a different shade of eyeliner can give you a pickup. (Confession: I wore blue eyeliner for years, until I read an article criticizing Princess Diana for doing so. Apparently, it's the worst color for blue eyes!)

Buy shoes in a bright color. I look for yellow shoes every spring, because they go with most other colors and make me feel like I'm wearing sunshine on my feet.

Occasionally allow yourself one small luxury—good earrings, a classy purse, above-average cologne. Don't let everything you own be secondhand, plain, or cheap.

Many of us don't exercise because of the "all-or-nothing" syndrome—we think we have to join a health club or jog every day, and we don't have the time or money for these things, so we do nothing and feel guilty! Actually, studies show that any exercise is better than none. Try incorporating exercise into your daily life—walk the kids to school, ride a bike to the library, do yard work. Even half an hour a day will do your body and spirit a lot of good.

Here's how my husband and I handle issues: We talk, early and often. We pray. We spend a lot of time together. We joke about things. For us, it's that simple. We just aren't geared to doing a set of exercises.

We have tried, however. A few years ago we went to a

Marriage Enrichment Weekend. We dutifully did the exercises, discussed the issues the speaker brought up. But when it was time to break for lunch we looked at each other and said, "Wanna leave?" I think we went out to eat, and that was it. We were happy; the thing wasn't for us.

How do you find what you love, what you're good at, and what you're not good at? Some of it is trial and error, or maybe *providence* and *grace*. We need to learn to listen closely to ourselves, to trust our feelings.

Is there something you find yourself returning to over and over? Or something you keep telling yourself you'll do—but somehow you never get around to it? Do you drown out *wishes* with *duties*? Do you keep saying yes to some involvement you think you *should* do—and wonder why you're not having fun yet?

I don't mean to say you should never try anything new "because it's not my gift." Obviously, you're sometimes going to be called on to perform some burdensome task; but, dear friend, all of life—even the Christian life—is not serving and self-sacrifice.

It is not selfish to think through who you are and what you enjoy and what you do well.

The Omnipresent *They*

Do you ever wonder who the *they* are that you worry about and what they think? Often enough they're brothers and sisters in Christ. Sometimes I think the deluge of Christian-advice books and tapes, seminars, radio shows, and magazines articles, is the worst thing to happen to some of us. We are already guilt-burdened, self-loathing. We might be better off reading an escapist novel, something fun. All the *shoulds* and *oughts* combine to impose a subtle but corrosive pressure, an inner voice that says, *You should conform to an ideal of the Christian woman.*

Here are some of the messages that come with the GECW syndrome that we mentioned earlier:

- Christian women are always in control of themselves, their families, their lives.
- Christian women are joyful!
- Christian women put their husbands and children before everything else.
- Christian women keep budgets, hold family devotions, tame their tongues, look for teachable moments, and don't have to work outside the home because they make all their kids' clothes and cook from scratch, thereby saving money.
- Christian women are content. They don't have dreams or doubts or restive longings.
- Christian women are always working to perfect themselves. They never blow anything off, never lounge around the house in jeans and a T-shirt.
- Christian women listen to the experts, most of whom are men.

How often have I heard women say, "I feel out of step with the women in my church. They all stay home, have little kids . . . are older, vote Republican . . . like to do counted cross-stitch . . . Name your conformity. Isn't it sad?

Of all places, the church should be a spiritual home where we feel safe and accepted, not judged—a home open to receiving the gifts and ideas of others. A place where we can go for that second doughnut, without the whole world pointing and staring in shocked horror.

We in the church speak of not conforming to worldly standards. But are there other, extra-biblical standards we're slaves to? Maybe we don't drink or smoke or go to R-rated movies. Great. We resist the pressures of the world . . . but we knuckle under to the peer pressure of the Christian community. We dismiss advice in secular magazines as unscriptural . . . but we say, "Pastor Know-It-All says it, I believe it, and that settles it." We read "Judge not . . ." and then go ahead and do exactly that.

I have friends who say, "I don't know *anyone* who looks like the women in the Christian magazines"—yet, like the

Perfect Mother, her shadow is long, her influence powerful. There are just enough women in our churches, neighborhoods, and schools who seem to come close enough to that ideal to make us feel depressed about never measuring up.

Women aren't alone in comparing themselves to others. Henri Nouwen is an esteemed Christian thinker who has served as a missionary and left a Harvard teaching post to minister to handicapped men at a community in Canada. He has lived a life of sacrificial service to others and devotion to God. Yet even he, who you'd think would be beyond such temptation, admits that he falls into the trap of comparison. He has observed that when another person receives an award or even a compliment, he himself feels somehow diminished. He was not honored; therefore, he must be unworthy. *Amazing.*

Learning to Laugh It Off

A sense of humor and some realistic self-talk works wonders. Incessant comparing is really adolescent: *She* has it, so I want it too! We need to take responsibility for ourselves and worry less about the other guy. More important, we really don't know what the other person is dealing with. That size-six woman in your Bible study, the one with the perfect house and honor-student children, may be struggling with menopause or a rocky marriage. We just don't know.

Our call is to *compassion*, not *comparison*.

If we view ourselves with sober judgment, we're less apt to be haunted by the specter of the perfect Christian woman. We grow in that firm sense of ourselves, and of what the Lord requires of us. We won't feel guilty about saying, "Yes, I am gifted in this area"; or, "No, I don't enjoy that." We can celebrate our accomplishments.

If we view ourselves *and others* with sober judgment, we can, like Paul, marvel at how God has given all of us different gifts. One body, many members. (Even the perfect

Christian woman has bad-hair days.)

Ask the Holy Spirit for wisdom to discern what God's Word is saying to you right now.

I won't say, "Throw out the self-help books. Don't listen to the experts." I *will* say: Read the Bible *before* you read the experts. Draw your own conclusions. Appropriate the Scripture's messages about joy, obedience, compassion, and wisdom for yourself. Notice how taking in God's Word drives out the negative voices.

When I spend a lot of time in Bible reading, I am incredibly healed. And challenged. I find myself writing my positive comments in the margins (I wish someone would publish a Bible with a lot of white space for those of us who like to do this). I don't always need someone to explain it all for me. The Holy Spirit is quite capable of speaking for himself.

After spending time with God, spend time with people who are gifted encouragers—cheerleaders, if you will. We in the church talk so much about sharing struggles and holding each other accountable, that I sometimes wonder if we haven't lost sight of the equally scriptural mandate to build one another up. Sometimes I don't want to be challenged by a friend. Sometimes I don't want to have my thoughts provoked. Sometimes I just want someone to laugh it off with me and offer me a doughnut. Good friends know that *you* know your weaknesses. They can affirm your strengths and encourage you to build on them. They can rejoice in you—just as you are. And you can do the same for them.

11

How to Fall Apart—and Pick Yourself Up Again

IT WAS ONE OF THOSE WEEKS. You've probably had them, too.

It was late November, and in our family that is Crazy Time: Thanksgiving, our wedding anniversary, Amanda's birthday, Christmas preparations. All at once. One year in particular the weather was also unremittingly awful. Sensing our frustration, our reliable Japanese car decided to fail its emissions test—right when we were going through one of our periodic cycles of poverty. Somewhere in there I suffered a major case of PMS, which, as you may know, strikes without warning. At such times I turn into a creature to which should be attached a sign: "Very Dangerous. Approach Cage at Your Own Risk." Not to be outdone, Amanda was going through a cantankerous period, and none of my parenting strategies seemed to be working.

I REALLY WANTED TO RUN AWAY FROM HOME!

I didn't, of course. I stood my ground and said to myself, "I *will* deal with these problems. I will solve them, work my way through. I am a Christian—therefore, I press on as I have been told to do."

Big mistake. I couldn't solve the weather, rebuild the

car's catalytic converter, move Christmas to another date, or do a thing about my hormones. I kept thinking things like, *How can I take over the World Bank? Maybe our marriage is over. Maybe I should send Amanda to military school. Maybe I should make another list . . .* You know—light, cheery thoughts like that. Of course this did wonders for my mood.

Have you ever seen a car stuck in the mud or the snow, and the driver is grinding the wheels, rocking back and forth, trying to get the thing out? That was me—trapped in a rut, going nowhere.

Sometimes the best way out of a rut is to kill the engine—back off from the problem for a while.

MAYBE A LITTLE SUNSHINE IS ALL YOU NEED

The other day I was out looking at the crocuses emerging in the garden. I felt great, and I wondered why. Nothing had changed; I still had too much to do and not enough time to do it. Then I realized that I had gotten a good night's sleep, it was the first pleasant day in months (after a long winter), and I had gone for a good walk.

Sometimes I think we underestimate the role of physical exercise and rest. Remember what your mother said about good, common sense. If you're feeling under pressure, ask yourself:

- Am I getting enough sleep?
- Am I suffering from cabin fever?
- Is the weather gray and depressing?
- Am I having enough fun, enjoyable diversions?
- Am I getting enough exercise?

Defying Common Logic

Of course the above tactic seems to go against everything we've been taught. The magazine articles tell you to *work* on *something* (implying it must be *you* and you have a problem to be solved). We've embraced the ideas that Christians never quit; Christians hang tough; Christians never complain. We're not supposed to "escape" from things.

Maybe not escape, but what about re-route?

Most of us have at least one headache in our lives that never seems to go away—no matter how much we pray about it, no matter how much we worry about it, no matter how hard we work at solutions. It could be a person we can't seem to get along with: our sister, our boss, our teenager. It could be finances, or a husband who has trouble holding down a job. It could be something we dislike in ourselves: a quick temper or a bad habit of procrastination. It could be a situation in which we are trying to help someone and nothing ever seems to change.

Most of us have runs, as I did, of "bad things happening to good people." One thing piles on another, and before you know it you feel like you're in a thicket of problems, trying to hack your way out.

You may be shouting, "That's me!" It's okay to feel frustrated. Acknowledge your pain. Don't feel like these things *shouldn't* get to you, as if you were some sort of bad Christian or emotional cripple when they do. Don't let your self-talk say to you, "Why am I complaining when people are starving in Africa?"

Even if we wouldn't dream of comparing our material possessions or achievements to others', we all occasionally rate our misery on a scale of misfortune. The Dear-Abby, positive-thinking response is something like, "Compared to the homeless, I have no problems," or "How can I complain about PMS? I'm not flat on my back."

Once I was griping to a friend about my usual assortment of woes. Then I stopped short. "I'm sorry, I shouldn't be talking like this. So many people have it worse than I do."

"No, it's okay," she said gently. "These things are important to *you*."

Can any of us judge another person's pain? We all have different stress thresholds. Some of us are deeply affected by the weather. Some have fluctuating hormones. Some are chronic worriers; others are not. I know a few women who are admirably easygoing. And just because we happen to be healthy, reasonably prosperous North Americans does not mean we, too, do not bleed when we are pricked.

So it's really all right to have a bad hour, a bad day. Go slump in your special chair, or throw yourself on the bed, or storm out of the house and walk. Call a friend. Do some physical work involving large motor movements. (Yanking up recalcitrant weeds is excellent.)

Defy the common logic that the Christian woman should never express strong negative emotion. We're told to make lemonade out of lemons. "A cheerful heart doeth good like a medicine." What about "Be angry, and sin not"?

Maybe you grew up never seeing your mother openly angry, and so you think it's something a nice girl doesn't do. You may have had a Christian camp counselor caution you about your "attitude" when you showed the slightest sign of discontent. Remember the Sunday school chorus: "I'm upright, downright happy all the time"? Ever notice the soloist in church who sings and smiles at the same time? (How do they do that?)

But joy in the Lord is a lot different from wearing a forced smile. Jesus wept and got angry. A good cry is a healthy thing, because tears help the body slough off accumulated toxins. A brief outburst of anger is a safety valve against the much more destructive hostility that can build up inside and eat away at us. Or, if we're not inclined that way, just admitting to ourselves, "This situation is incredibly frustrating and I feel down about it" can be a step in the right direction—a step toward killing the engine and getting out of the rut.

After we do that, though, it's time to reroute.

ARE YOU A CONTROL-AHOLIC?

Many women load themselves up with unnecessary stress because they need to be in control of their environment, other people, and every situation they find themselves in. Then, when life spins out of their control—as it invariably will—they're unable to cope. You may be a "control-aholic" if you . . .

- Never do anything spontaneous
- Fall apart when your schedule is interrupted
- Have to look just right every time you go out (or even if you're not going out)
- Yell at your children excessively about messing up the house (We've heard of women who vacuum up footprints on the carpet.)
- Have to have everything matching
- Spend an inordinate amount of time on planning, organizing, and seeking to emulate that seemingly-perfect friend
- Need to know exactly what to expect of a given event or circumstance
- Can't relax until "all the work is done"
- Feel uncomfortable with mystery, randomness, unanswered questions (Many control-aholics have a need to make sense out of everything, including complex spiritual issues.)

Draw Another Map

Think about the problems in your life that never seem to get resolved: Have you considered walking away from them for a while, backing off, and taking a completely different approach?

This is hard for women to do. We usually cast ourselves in the role of *rescuer, solver, coper*. We can't see that sometimes our intervention—and the accompanying frustration—might be making matters worse.

I know a woman whose husband couldn't seem to find his vocational niche. His "big dream" led him, alternately, to sell real estate, raise money for a Christian college, and to start his own business. Somehow the big dream kept changing. At one point, he enrolled in seminary to study for the ministry, but eventually decided—after a couple of years and several thousand dollars—that the pastorate wasn't for him. Through all this his wife was working full time as a nurse. She loved her husband and wanted to see him achieve his big dream. She tried to help him in all kinds of ways, from offering advice to putting him through seminary. At the same time, she was becoming more and more resentful of her role as the strong, helpful wife. Finally she realized that all her efforts were only contributing to the problem. She decided to back off, affirm him for who he was beyond whatever job he happened to have . . . and leave the rest up to God.

It worked! Today her husband has found a job that seems to fulfill him, and she has cut back to part-time hospice nursing. By rerouting, she broke out of a cycle of frustration.

Rerouting is a life skill we can implement in many different situations. It can help us enormously to deal with stress, because when we reroute we *separate the problem from our frustration about the problem*. This is critical, because when something seems unsolvable for a long period of time, we can get so frustrated that we lose sight of what the original issue was. A lower-case problem becomes a capital PROBLEM.

Ask yourself these questions:

- What's my "problem that won't go away"? What's really grinding on me right now?
- Are my efforts at solving things making matters worse, deepening the rut?
- Has my frustration magnified the issue? Are things as bad as they seem?
- What do I stand to lose by giving this one up? What do I stand to gain?

As I've told you before, we've gone through periodic cycles of financial stress at our house. We're not incompetent at managing money, but neither is Ron Blue going to use us as a model couple in this area. Our approach to the problem used to be panic, followed by the edict from one of us: "We have to sit down and TALK." (Aren't those money talks fun?) We'd usually wind up in an argument and go our separate ways feeling worse than ever, with no perceptible increase in the family exchequer.

Eventually I decided I was sick of the arguments, sick of the worry . . . and I didn't want to get sick *from* the worry. It came to me that such preoccupation with money worries was even unspiritual. God *would* provide. He always had, and by focusing too much on finances I wasn't focusing on the things that really mattered. My husband and I had made certain choices—among them, to pursue Christian work *and* live in an area with good schools, safe streets, (and therefore high taxes). Such choices almost ensured we would always have to live frugally, and we had to live with the consequences of those choices.

When I gave up my *spin-the-wheels* approach to dealing with money, I felt a tremendous burden being lifted from me. I was rerouting even before I learned the term.

Sometimes You Need to Back Out

Sometimes it's really difficult to give up a problem. That's especially true if we feel we're trying to help someone. Perhaps there's a neighbor family you're dealing with. They're beset by poverty, chronic illness, and various other malfunctions and misfortunes. You may have taken it upon yourself to do their shopping, help clean their house, mind their wandering children. But you're frustrated, because nothing ever seems to improve for them and they seem unable or unwilling to help themselves. You're beginning to think that you've taken on too much and maybe it's time for a social worker to step in—if they'd let her in the house.

Maybe you do need to start extricating yourself. Maybe *your* family needs more of you. Are there others who could help as effectively? What do you lose by giving up this frustration? A sense of yourself as a person who goes the extra mile? You've already got a hard-earned star in your crown! What will you gain? A load off your mind? More time? Isn't that important too?

You may not be burdened with one ongoing problem, but we all have bad weeks or months when we experience "frustration pileup," the accumulation of little naggy irritations that collectively can send us hunting for a person-sized burrow to hide in.

If you're running into a frustration pileup, try this: First, try a change of scenery—maybe the library or a peaceful spot in the church. Or really pamper yourself, and go to a nice coffee shop for capuccino and a sticky cinnamon roll. Then, count your frustrations. Name them one by one. Try to be somewhat dispassionate ("I hate my life" is not a helpful analysis). Ask yourself: Which of these will simply go away with time? Which of these is *really* bothering me? What can I live with? Laugh off? What else might be going on right now that's stressing me out? Am I getting enough sleep? Eating right most of the time? Exercising? What about that virus I had last month? Maybe it's still lingering.

Exercises like this help us back out of and *distance* ourselves from our irritations, thus cutting them down to size. (And they're a good excuse to eat something that's irrelevant: "I have to have a sweet roll because I'm analyzing my frustrations.")

We can also reroute by literally walking away from something. Marital counselors know the value of interrupting an escalating argument with a cooling-off period, when one spouse might say, "I don't want to deal with this right now. I think we need to stop this before it gets any worse, so I'm going to take a walk." It might be a *long* walk, but in all likelihood he won't return as angry as before.

The same principle can apply to exchanges with our children. Kids grow to expect us to respond in predictable ways. Usually when Amanda dawdles, I scold and hover: "Hurry up!" She then reacts by moving even more slowly. I lose my temper, and the situation deteriorates. But if I *don't* scold, if I smile and calmly say, "Do the best you can; I'm going to go do the breakfast dishes"—I catch her off guard. She may even get her socks and shoes on in less than five minutes.

Smoothly . . . Smoothly

Another way to reroute is to dial down the intensity. So many of us women take things so personally, so emotionally. We go around living at this fever pitch. Possibly because of those powerful brain connections, we can't shrug anything off. Everything becomes larger than life. (Recurring exchange between my mate and me: "It isn't important," he says. "It *is* important!" I snap.)

Our children misbehave and it reflects on our mothering. Our house is cluttered and we simply can't stand it one minute longer; we attack the mess. We have a bad-hair day or a fat day and decide we're not fit to be seen in public. Even our movements become frenetic, a constant bustle. Life loses its smoothness and the ride gets bumpy.

I've heard of people who were literally addicted to this intensity. Somehow the drama gave them an emotional high they craved. It's very bad for you to live like this. Besides, when *everything* is important, *nothing* is important—in other words, we lose the ability to discern between the insignificant and what really does deserve our attention.

Listen to your interactions with others. What do they sound like? Does your voice get an edge to it when you talk to your husband or children? Are you a yeller? Do you regularly exaggerate in your conversation with friends, blow everything out of proportion? At one time or another we all do one or more of these things. It's when they get to be a reflexive habit that we need to back off, because if we act *as if* there's a problem, we can create a problem where none existed before.

One way to smooth out the rough spots and deal with this *larger-than-life* mentality is to make sure we're getting enough fun in our lives. That's not as trivial as it sounds. We all need areas of our life where no one wants anything from us except our companionship, where we can laugh and let down our hair and forget our burdens for a while. Everything doesn't always have to be serious and purposeful. We all know that Christians don't have to go around with long faces, but we don't always act like it. "The couples with kids at my church always seem so serious," observed a newlywed recently. "They never seem to be having any fun." Does it sound like you?

I won't tell you *how to have fun*, although I've given some suggestions in the boxes scattered throughout this book. Fun to me is what happens when I break out of my normal routine. Sure, writing is fun for me—but it's also work. Church can be fun—but it's also serious and challenging. It's fun when I get away from the computer and walk Amanda home from school (there's a whole book to be written on really enjoying your kids). It's fun when I can play word games with friends. It's fun when we go to my mother's and we all watch a video, like *Father of the Bride*. It's even fun to go to my beauty salon and sit under the dryer while I read *People* magazine (and realize how many current celebrities I've never heard of)!

PLAN NOT TO PLAN

Every once in awhile, it's healthy to lay low, especially during those times when you'd ordinarily be swamped with activity—the Christmas holidays, the end-of-school rush. You might plan for a low-key holiday—letting your family eat what they want, when they want to. Or, don't make any plans or commitments for a week. Wear your robe all morning, eat nothing but fruit for dinner, take a long bath, play word games. "Downscaling" activity is a great way to recharge your batteries.

When we have enough lightness, even play, in our lives, it provides an important safety valve for tensions, puts things into perspective, and also gets us into the habit of not taking everything—including ourselves—so seriously. Every now and then, stop and check yourself: Have I had any fun lately? When? If not, how could I set aside some time to just kick back and enjoy myself? (I'm still working on this one myself.)

The Best Map

When it comes right down to it, Scripture is the best road map for rerouting. "Do not be anxious about anything, but in everything, by prayer and petition, with thanksgiving, present your requests to God. And the peace of God, which transcends all understanding, will guard your hearts and your minds in Christ Jesus" (Phil. 4:6–7). The Bible is full of passages on God's care for us, on seeking His peace, on wisdom and discernment. When you come to God's Word thirsty for a word of comfort or insight, it's startling how some passages can immediately grab you with their relevance: *Yes! That's exactly what I'm dealing with!*

Depend on it: *We will run head on into frustration pileups.* One problem may go away, only to be replaced by another. (One thing I always appreciate about Scripture is its healthy realism about the fallen human condition.) But we can rely on a gracious God to get us through.

The God who allows us to face our own limits and to fall apart is the God who wants to catch us as we fall. He's great at putting back together all that's fallen apart.

Let go, and let Him remake.

12

Take Your Dreams Out of the Closet!

DO YOU HAVE A BIG, secret dream? Something that keeps welling up inside, but you keep shoving it down, saying, "Later, later"? Maybe you've always wanted to start a home business. Maybe you'd like to finish your interrupted college education; test yourself on a rugged wilderness trip; start a shelter for abused women in your town.

Perhaps you're artistic, like my friend Dori, who when she entered her fifties decided to take up painting seriously. Or, like another friend, Bobette, you're interested in Christian service and are considering seminary.

Maybe you feel like you're not in a rut but a *chasm*, and you'd like to make some *big* change—go on a once-and-for-all diet, find a new job, get to know a new circle of friends.

Small refreshers are important, but there comes a time when we have to look at the big picture. We need growth and change and challenge to feel fully alive, to feel we're seeking and then fulfilling God's purpose for us.

Open That Treasure Chest

Are the pressures of children and chores starting to pile up? Are you frustrated by the endless minutiae of daily

SHOULD YOU DECIDE TO ACCEPT IT . . .

Your first mission here on earth is to seek out and find, in daily—even hourly—communication, the one from whom your mission is derived. Your second mission is to do what you can, moment by moment, day by day, step by step, to make this world a better place, following the leading and guidance of God's Spirit within you and around you. Your third mission is one which is uniquely yours, and that is: To exercise the talent that you particularly came to earth to use—your greatest gift, that which you most delight to use; in the places or settings God has caused to appeal to you the most; and for those purposes that God most needs to have done in the world.

—Richard Nelson Bolles

To put it more concisely:
The place God calls you to is the place where your deep gladness and the world's deep hunger meet.

—Frederick Buechner

living? Do you feel spiritually dry? Do you secretly think, *There's got to be more than this?* Or maybe you're basically content with your life, but you're in a holding pattern. You've been doing essentially the same things for several years and you're wondering if you need some sort of long-range goal, some vision for the future.

You do. So what's stopping you? Are you saying, "I can't reach for my dreams until: 1) the kids are through college; 2) we've paid off our bills; 3) I can find the time; 4) I've got my mother settled in her new apartment; 5) I can quit my job; 6) I'm thin; 7) the ozone hole closes up"?

You can always find an excuse to postpone your life. But if you put your dreams in the closet for too long they may get moth-eaten. Dreams are treasures that we store away for *later use*—not to be buried and forgotten.

"But I've got little kids and can't afford a sitter," you protest. "How realistically can I pursue something?" Or, "We can't make ends meet unless I work. How can you help me? Where do I start?"

Love God, and then do what you like. —St. Augustine

You have to *start small* but *think big*.

Start small: When I quit my job to stay home and write, it was no overnight decision. I had known for years that I was headed in that direction; but I also knew I had to be patient, hone my skills, cultivate contacts, get published in visible places . . . and wait on God's timing. A decade ago, before my daughter was born, I was toiling away in public relations. I figured the experience would be useful, and it was; but I also knew it wasn't where I wanted to spend my life. Whenever I felt frustrated in my work I told myself, *Be patient. You're planting seeds for the future.*

Much of what happened was not my doing. God sent encouragers and counselors along the way. Still, it took years of seed-sowing, of patience, of seeking the Lord's leading to bring me to the place where I felt ready to take the big risk. I kept having the dream I told you about—of a bird starving in her cage. I knew what it meant, and it bothered me that I wasn't able to feed her. Finally the time came when God simply said, "Go."

And I went.

"But I have raised you up for this very purpose, that I might show you my power and my name might be honored in all the earth" (Exo. 9:16). "For we are God's workman-

145

ship, created in Christ Jesus to do good works, which God prepared in advance for us to do" (Eph. 2:10).

Think big: For what purpose has God raised you up? What good works has He prepared you for?

Who's Gold Vessel Are You?

We are God's workmanship. God has gifted us with special talents and inclinations and interests to be used to His glory. There's a special delight when this happens—and when it doesn't, contributions to His kingdom are lost, and it's a tragedy.

I recently read of a nineteenth-century author named Rebecca Harding Davis. I had never heard of her. Rebecca had dreams and ideas, a fierce desire to write of what she had observed growing up in the industrial town of Wheeling, West Virginia. She produced a few short stories, and one widely acclaimed novel about life among the poor mill-workers of the era, an *Uncle Tom's Cabin* for the Industrial Revolution. Critics hailed her writings as equal to that of Nathaniel Hawthorne. But Rebecca was an upper-class wife and mother—with a certain social position to be maintained. Her own needs and longings were to be laid aside in favor of those of her family. She succumbed to the prevailing social pressures, and her gifts were lost to us.

Today, cultural expectations are quite different, but I suspect there are some Rebeccas out there—wanting to try, to learn, to grow, but fearful of taking the leap. Others may not have even considered "the importance of significance."

Believe me when I say that God has something for you. Something significant. There is some contribution that you alone can make to the kingdom of God. Something that stretches and challenges and exhilarates you—something that feels *true*. When you find it, you will come to the end of the day and say with satisfaction, "I did something today that really mattered." But first, you have to give yourself permission to seek it.

Let me be very clear about something here. I am *not* saying that it isn't significant to rear children, love and make a home for a husband and family, hold down an honorable job, or serve in your church. All of these things are wonderful and right and good. But there can come a time in our lives, for some of us anyway, when we long for something more . . . something that is uniquely our own. It is important that you feel your life is *moving* somewhere, toward a goal, toward a dream. There's nothing worse than the feeling that you are stuck, on hold, stalled in a cul-de-sac.

OF WEASELS AND WOMEN

In *Teaching a Stone to Talk*, essayist Annie Dillard writes about observing weasels. The weasel, she says, grasps his prey by the throat or at the base of the skull and simply does not let go. The weasel, Dillard says, "lives as he's meant to." So, she says, can we: "The thing is to stalk your calling in a certain skilled and supple way, to locate the most tender and live spot and plug into that pulse . . . yielding at every moment to the perfect freedom of single necessity." Do you have a "single necessity," something you leap at and hold onto for dear life?

Practically speaking, what could you do with that ten or twenty percent of time available to you to pursue your goal, dream, course of study? You could take a class. Most areas have a community college or liberal-arts institution that welcomes "older" students. You could even audit a course, and save yourself the pressure of making a certain grade. Or, if more schooling doesn't appeal to you, you could read on your own about your area of interest. The library is a great getaway!

Maybe you are a person who prefers hands-on volunteer work. Even a small amount of time will be gratefully received. Don't underestimate the experience such work can give you; volunteers can become skilled in management, fund-raising techniques, counseling, media relations—all sorts of areas. It's important, however, to focus your efforts on something you're really interested in. Take your volunteer work seriously, using your unique, individual gifts. Don't limit yourself to the approved "Christian causes," as important as they are. If you love animals, for example, why not work at a wildlife refuge that rehabilitates injured creatures?

If you are artistic, you could make pastel portraits of your friends' children, or design banners for your church. If you like to write, set yourself a goal of publishing an article once a quarter. Allow yourself an hour a day to play the piano if you are musically inclined. The options are almost limitless, if you will think through what you would like to do, and then allow yourself that liberty.

Are You Sabotaging Yourself?

Whatever your situation, you need to think hard about the roadblocks you may be throwing up. Do you really have "no time"? Do your children really need you twenty-four hours a day, or could your husband take over one evening so that you could take a class? What are you doing while the kids are in school? How are you using your lunch breaks at work?

In addition to starting small, but thinking big, there's a spiritual component to challenging yourself. It has to do with reconnecting to yourself, and in so doing, reconnecting with the God who loves you.

We can sabotage ourselves by narrowing our horizons, limiting ourselves to family and home and church and (maybe) a job. We can forget what it was like before we had

YOU CALL THE SHOTS

An increasing number of women (and men) are finding that working at home, for themselves, is a rewarding alternative to the office grind, especially in today's uncertain economic climate. Freelance writing, child care, and home typing are some of the more common work-at-home jobs, but there are others:

• Become a representative for Shaklee, Beauty for All Seasons, Jafra, Discovery Toys, or one of the many other companies that sell through home parties or one-on-one sales contacts.

• If you have nursing skills, consider becoming an independent consultant in a health-care area. One woman I know works as a lactation consultant, helping new mothers with breastfeeding problems. Someone with an insurance background could hire herself out to help people through the Medicare maze.

• Make personalized greeting cards.

• Create a service that delivers gourmet meals to people's homes.

• Help other home workers—with storage organization, computer problems, accounting advice.

• Become a gardening consultant.

• Create and market educational software for homeschoolers.

• Consider becoming involved in some aspect of "elder care." (The fastest-growing segment of our population are people over eighty-five. Quite a few of them are in their own homes, and would be willing to pay for small services.)

these responsibilities, when all of life seemed open to us. It can even seem wrong somehow for a Christian woman to want to explore too much.

But explore we must. One February, my husband and I

were walking along the shores of Lake Michigan. It was a blustery day; the sky was full of wind-driven clouds that seemed to meet the churning, whitecapped waters. In the midst of the mighty sea stood massive ice formations. It could have been Alaska or the west coast of Ireland. The wind and the waves and the sky blew into my soul, touching something inherent, exposing something deep. I have almost never felt closer to God—closer to something in myself. I love the water; I love bracing myself against challenging weather. I think about the long-gone sailors who pitted themselves against the storms of Lake Michigan— and sometimes lost. I love the feeling that God is so big, there's just more and more to know about Him, and I want to spend a lifetime finding out.

The feeling that day was so overwhelming, I wept—the way you sometimes weep when you read something that hits you with its gut-level truth.

Another, more cozy, time, I was dusting books, something I do about twice a year. I sat on the floor with my dust rag, wiping out the shelves; picking up my well-loved "friends" and gently cleaning them. I *love* handling books, especially hardcovers. I love their smell and texture, the various kinds of paper and typefaces used. I think it would be interesting to collect rare hand-bound titles, products of the bookmaker's art.

If you handle books, you will start reading them. I leafed through some titles I hadn't looked at in years, books I had bought in college, or high school—books that had meant something to me at the time. Do you remember the feeling when you were seventeen or eighteen and discovered an author or an idea for the first time? There's nothing quite like it. As I went through these old friends, I remembered the girl I had been, and I was suddenly nostalgic. Where had that girl gone?

She's still there, somewhere under all the layers. But good Christian wives and mothers have obligations. They're supposed to know all the answers. Can they still be as searching, as vulnerable, as they were at eighteen? Wouldn't these books be a waste of time now?

My daughter, then a toddler, came bounding into my reverie. But the feeling had already taken hold. It was similar to what I had felt on the winter beach: This, too, is me.

Struck by a Bolt Out of the Blue

Maybe you've had a similar experience and didn't quite know what to do with it. You don't exactly plan for it. Nor does it fit into some five-year goal-setting scheme. What it *does* is give you a surer sense of yourself; it deepens you, sensitizes you, points you to what *could be*.

This is one reason why it's so important to regularly take time for yourself. It is in solitude that we have the freedom to not live up to anyone else's expectations of us. We have the quiet to listen to that inner voice—and to learn to trust that voice. And then the bolt strikes from the blue.

We also need to allow ourselves the leisure, the *re-creation*, out of which these experiences spring. I had my "beach epiphany" when I was taking a long weekend at my mother-in-law's. When you're feeling rested, when you're enjoying a change of scenery, you release creativity, playfulness, imagination. Encrustations of humdrum routine fall away and the result is a free spirit.

Things of great beauty can also have this enlarging, almost ennobling effect. I confess, I'm something of a traditionalist when it comes to the music of the church. I love a soaring Bach organ prelude. I cry when we sing "O Holy Jesus, How Hast Thou Offended?" on Good Friday. My spine tingles when the choir sings Handel's "And the Glory of the Lord Shall Be Revealed" at Christmastime. But put a soloist at the mike with an amplified backup tape, and it's not the same. There are many contemporary praise songs that make me feel like I'm talking to God; Bach and

Handel feel like God bending down to me.

To challenge yourself also means to stretch your brain; to actively seek beauty. There is so much in the world that is pointless and banal. Ridiculous TV sitcoms. Boring architecture. Unexamined ideas. Music produced by machines. Offensive celebrities. Unfortunately, we Christians aren't immune to this mediocrity. But we, of all people, should seek that which is true, noble, pure, lovely (Phil. 4:8). Look for the things that lift, that, like the spires of Gothic cathedrals, point toward heaven. Read good literature that inspires, expands your mind, even if it's Shakespeare or a Russian novel. Take an architectural tour of your city. Subscribe to an intellectually demanding magazine. (Maybe one you don't always agree with.)

Enjoy the out of doors. Nature is never banal. Especially the big picture—mountains, oceans, deserts. If you don't live near these natural sights, you may have to settle for the next best thing. A couple of years ago, our family visited the aquarium in downtown Chicago. It had recently acquired several beluga whales. They are relatively small creatures, white, and always seeming to wear a smile. We greeted them, and they performed for us. I couldn't take my eyes off these wonders of God's creation!

After the porpoise performance ended, the crowd drifted over and pressed close to the whale tank. I watched the expressions on people's faces. They were peaceful. Almost saintly. I felt much as I do when I listen to Handel: enlarged, challenged to be *better*. God has so many ways of showing himself.

What Are You Afraid Of?

To seek God's purpose for us, we have to ask why we don't challenge ourselves more. Are we afraid of failure? Success? What people will think? Upsetting the applecart? Changing our children's routine? Do we think that it is somehow wrong to claim anything for ourselves?

Women are traditionally the stable anchors of the home, not the questing voyagers. It has been the man's job to tramp the streets for employment and bring the bread home. Women made sure there was wood on the fire and food on the table. If you read the biographies of famous artists, authors, scientists of the past, you will see that these men generally had down-to-earth wives who kept their mates fed and in clean socks and underwear. (Dr. and Mrs. Einstein are just one example.) It has been unseemly for women to want adventure.

There aren't a great number of models of Christian wives and mothers who challenged themselves and sought to do something big for God. But here are some, to mention a few: Nancy Judson, pioneer missionary to Burma. Catherine Booth, mother of the Salvation Army. Harriet Beecher Stowe, the "little lady" whose book inflamed a nation. Catherine Marshall LeSourd, the young widow who discovered her gift of writing. Joy Davidman Lewis, the late-in-life convert who married and matched wits with C. S. Lewis. Coretta Scott King, wife of the famous civil rights leader. Dr. Roberta Hestenes, president of Eastern College.

You may find models closer to home, right in your community. If you dreamed as a young person of becoming a missionary doctor, and missed that opportunity, all is not lost. Maybe there is a Christian doctor who could use some part-time help. You can still achieve a little piece of that dream. You could be the encourager and organizer that doctor hasn't had. This simply gives you an idea of what can be done to fulfill what you would like to do.

Another common reason why women don't challenge themselves is the fear of appearing selfish. I read an article awhile ago in *Leadership*, the journal for pastors, that explained the difference between being "wholly ambitious" and "holy ambition." The point was made that not all ambition is ungodly. Holy ambition means that we want to achieve for the Kingdom; that we, as God's workmanship,

THANK YOU, LEONARD LESOURD

Dreaming big doesn't necessarily mean you start big. The meteoric rise to the top, complete with accompaniment from the Rocky soundtrack, is nearly always the stuff of fiction. Dreams are wonderful, and they can be the engine that drives you to reach a goal, but without the plodding, unglamorous, intentional steps to implement them, they too often remain only enticing fancies.

When I was in college, I realized I wanted to work with words—somehow. And I wanted to reach people—somehow. But I didn't start by writing books. I wrote book reviews for one of the Chicago newspapers, to the tune of about $35 apiece. This gave me the confidence to think, Maybe I do have something to offer. But still, the timing wasn't right; also, I had to make a living. So I got a job in public relations. I knew I didn't want to write glowing copy about someone else's work forever, but it was good experience. I knew God was working, planting seeds that would eventually flower.

A critical breakthrough came when I was at home with a new baby, wondering where God was leading me. I still had the dream. Something, I don't remember what, led me to write Leonard LeSourd, former editor of Guideposts, one of the deans of Christian publishing and husband of the late Catherine Marshall. In effect I asked him, "I want to write. What would you advise?"

I was thrilled to receive a letter back on impressive stationery. He very graciously advised me to establish a base with a publication that would use my work frequently, thus giving me visibility and a reliable outlet. I had never thought of it!

That was a turning point for me. I joined the staff of a Christian magazine that offered me lots of opportunities to write and get to know people in the business, but it was seven more years before I was able to make one big dream come true—the dream of staying at home, writing books, and speaking. Seven years of building. Seven years of crystallizing exactly what my dream, my calling, was.

feel compelled to be obedient by stewarding the gifts He has given us and using them for good. Contrarily, the wholly ambitious person seeks to glorify him or herself—sometimes in the guise of wanting to serve the Lord.

Does holy ambition scare you? Have you ever considered that maybe the world needs what you have to offer? Perhaps the less selfish way is to give something to a dying world.

Seek Significance

The evangelical community does not always encourage women who seek significance, so you may have to do some digging. Write to a well-known woman in a field you're interested in. If you attended a Christian college, you could write to a woman professor. If you're interested in teaching parent education to underprivileged mothers, for instance, and you hear a woman on Christian radio who has a ministry doing just that, get in touch with her. Most Christian women in leadership are happy to be asked advice, to encourage their sisters in any way they can. If calling someone intimidates you, get together with other women with similar aspirations.

No matter what other pursuits women may have, they are invariably drawn back to the home and family. This is good, normal, commendable. But as I have said before, we all need a balance. I cover the balance of "nesting and soaring" in my book *The Woman With Two Heads*. We don't really help our families when we do it all for them. Children must learn to pitch in with chores, take responsibility. And most husbands would be happy to help out in the kitchen, for example, if they were just given a little instruction.

The stereotype of the man who can't boil water or change a diaper is fast fading—thanks be to God! Many husbands applaud the chance for their wives to grow, to seek a dream. But, if you've been at home for a number of years, you may have to sit down with your family and outline specifically what it will mean for you to go back to school, work outside the home, or take on a major volunteer involvement.

The last barrier to finding and doing your dream is simple inertia. Why *should* you challenge yourself? You're content with your life as it is . . . pretty much.

Remember that successful ventures are those that look to the future, whose proponents ask, "What can we do better?" They don't rest on their laurels. We should be continually asking ourselves, "How is God working in me right now?" Let Him do something new: "See, I am doing a new thing! Now it springs up; do you not perceive it? I am making a way in the desert and streams in the wasteland" (Isa. 43:19).

Most important: *Believe that God will direct and empower you.* "For God did not give us a spirit of timidity . . ." (2 Tim. 1:7). Change is frightening. Claiming something for ourselves is scary, especially if we're not used to doing it. But God has given us a spirit of love and power and self-discipline—"holy boldness," if you will—that enables us to conquer the fear, and equips us to take up a new challenge.

Now What?

How do we find out what the Lord may have for us, if there isn't something that readily comes to mind? Every new direction begins with prayer—committing your questions and concerns to the Lord. Even if you already feel led in a certain direction, pray anyway. Seek confirmation from others. If you have discerned God's leading accurately, He will give you peace and will help smooth the way. Even if the call is sure, your timing and God's may be different. I wanted to launch my writing career long before it actually happened. It was a great lesson in patience, waiting upon the Lord.

Read the Bible. Notice that God says "Go and do" to His people more often than "Stay." Reread Hebrews 11, and be inspired by all that our spiritual forefathers did by faith.

Return again to the stories of Abraham and Sarah, Jacob, Moses, Deborah, Samuel, Ruth, Isaiah. Mary and her cousin Elizabeth, Paul and Peter. God calls you to step out just as He called them.

Maybe your thing is not an occupational or professional venture. I know a mother of young children who volunteers at a local crisis pregnancy center, and is looking forward to the day when she can be involved in a more significant way. That is a task that will affect generations. It is a "big thing" in God's eyes.

Yours may be a physical adventure—mountain climbing or whitewater rafting. After her husband passed away, poet Luci Shaw and a friend sailed across Lake Michigan, partly for the sheer challenge of it. Such adventures can be life-altering experiences.

Is there something you've always wanted to learn? Another language? Calligraphy? Economics? How to cook classic French cuisine? Such knowledge can lead to a career, but it doesn't have to. The joy is in the challenge and the personal growth. And anything, if you do it with excellence, thanking God for the opportunity He has given you, can be offered back to Him as a gift.

No Gifts?—Give It Up!

You may be saying about now, "But I have no special talents." Everyone has talent, my friend, it just may take someone else to point it out to you. My mother is gifted in interpersonal relationships. I'd say it's her greatest skill. She has had a successful career in public relations and fund-raising for almost twenty years, and her success is more a result of her people skills than any technical abilities.

Someone else may be compassionate. Or meticulous. Or insatiably curious. All these qualities can be used in some significant capacity. There are a number of vocational-assessment tests you can take to determine where your abilities might be best used. (A friend of mine took one, and the analysis told her she would make an excellent mortician! Oh, well.)

You have to declare, "Yes! I have something to offer the Kingdom!" We're all vessels, being shaped for God's use. That's how He works. And in some mysterious way, even our imperfections don't hinder Him from completing His purposes.

God's purpose for you may be to explore some professional passion. It's wonderful when you can make a living doing what you love. But again, this is where fear can get in the way for women. I've known several who had remarkable talents and had considered taking the professional plunge, but they hung back—fearing the unknown. No one had ever encouraged them to "go for it," and (this is crucial) they didn't see themselves as achievers.

There's a strong bias against working women in some sectors of the church today. Even women who do have jobs are quick to say they have them because they need the money, not because they enjoy working. Surveys of employed Christian women (two-thirds of us) show that the majority don't think of their work as a "career."

Despite the glamorous media images of women as high-powered lawyers and executives, many have tedious, unglamorous jobs. And although some statistics purport that women are entering the work force in droves, the fact is, those numbers include women who work part time or even seasonally.

If, however, you feel led to a career that is also a calling, a true vocation—then out of obedience, you must heed that leading. Enlist the support of your family. Find a group of like-minded Christian women with whom you can share your joys and struggles. Hire a cleaning service if necessary (or a teenager)! The more at peace you feel about your decision, the less likely you are to be defensive when your choice is criticized. The same applies to women who choose to stay at home.

Many of us have a "neglected bird" within. God will give us the courage, and the resources, to open up the treasure chest of our forgotten dreams. It won't be easy, but doing the hard thing, the *best* thing, is exhilarating.

So, go for it. God will bless you on the journey!

13

Making Peace With Where You've Been, Looking Forward to Where You're Going

IN THE BEGINNING OF THIS BOOK, I shared with you how difficult it was for me to lose my dad. How I stepped back and thought about where I was going, what I would do with the next few decades of my life, how I could build on Dad's legacy.

I didn't tell you what that legacy was.

There was a time, when I was younger, that my dad and I didn't always see eye-to-eye. He had a hot temper and didn't always express himself tactfully enough to satisfy a sensitive adolescent. The volume level in our house when I was growing up was sometimes pretty intense. Meanwhile, my mother—as mothers often do—served as the buffer, the placater, the mediator. When the term "dysfunctional family" surfaced a few years ago, I wondered if mine had been one.

Maybe it was, maybe it wasn't. In one important way it doesn't matter. Now that I'm a parent, I realize that my parents were doing the best they could, given their temperaments, dreams, disappointments, backgrounds. Maybe they even did better than average: My three siblings and I are all happily married and reasonably responsible adults. My father—how I miss him—left a remarkable legacy of marital fidelity, personal honesty, and artistic talent; of humor and insight and a sense of what it was to be a struggling human being. My mother, still well and thriving, recently announced that she intends to sell the family home and move a thousand miles away to the seashore!

SOFTENING THE SOIL OF YOUR HEART

We're so attached to the idea that all situations have to be resolved right now that sometimes we forget that we need to let God do the resolving—which may take time.

If there is a particularly difficult person in your life, someone you find it hard to forgive, or are alienated from in some way, the best way to deal with this person may not be confrontation or even speaking the truth in love. Certainly don't cut yourself off from him or her, but continue to interact casually with the person, at work, in church, or at family gatherings. While you are doing this, maintain an attitude of good will and good intention toward the person even though the glitch in your relationship is not resolved.

Pray that God will help you let the matter go—or at least help you to hold it loosely ("at the end of a long rope," as someone has put it), while He softens the soil of your heart and plants a seed that may eventually flower into reconciliation and restoration of the relationship.

I guess you could say I've made peace with my past—something we all have to do if we are to be truly emotionally free. Like Dad, I'm *trying* to make peace with my fallibility—something we all have to come to terms with. I also hope I can emulate my mother, who seeks growth and challenge the way a hummingbird seeks nectar.

Making peace with the idea of my mother moving halfway across the country is something else again . . .

Getting On With Life

If we're to unload the guilt and the stress, to flower into the women God has created us to be, we have to deal with our past, accept our humanness, and look to the future with a sense of hope, anticipation.

We've talked of ways to find time for yourself, make a special place for yourself, overcome guilt, simplify your life. We haven't really addressed *stepping out of* your life for a time—I mean, getting away and taking a hard look at where you've been and where you're going. Sometimes we have to actually go away to get that perspective.

You could take an overnight trip—or better yet, a long weekend—and go to a hotel, a retreat center, even a convent or monastery. Your husband, mother, or friend will look after your children for you. Get out of reach for a while. Get a room all to yourself. (Doesn't it sound inviting?) Pack your Bible, some good books, a journal. (If you don't keep a journal, this may be a good time to start one.) Read, pray, relax, rest. Go for walks, soak up the quiet.

If this isn't an option for you, or for some reason is not appealing, why not encourage your *family* to take a long weekend and leave you alone in your home? Maybe your husband could take the kids to Grandma's, or camping. (I say, let them rough it while you bask in solitary comfort.) Go to another church where you don't know anyone. Use the time wisely, if you stay at home. It's a retreat, not a chance to get caught up on chores!

If you're struggling to make peace with your past, a retreat is an excellent way to take time to reflect, especially if your past has bequeathed an inheritance of guilt and perfectionism. We all know people who got the message growing up that, "Christians are always victorious."

(Translated: Christians never fail). Some were asked repeatedly, "What would Jesus do in this situation?" (The child thinks, *But I'm not Jesus. I'm just a little kid.* But she doesn't dare challenge the question.)

Maybe you grew up thinking God was a legalistic cop. When you brought home a report card with A's and B's, you were greeted with, "Couldn't you do better than this?" Others have known an environment of "frozen rage"—controlled, unexpressed hostility that always wore a smile.

Most of us stumble out of childhood carrying some sort of baggage. But there comes a time when we have to drop that baggage—stop running away from our past, and start progressing toward peace.

If you had a less than desirable upbringing, it may help to realize that your parents may have received some of the same messages in their childhood that they transmitted to you. It might be time to recognize that they could have been struggling against insurmountable odds. Even if they were Christians, they didn't have the benefit of Christian counselors, recovery books, child-rearing manuals, and ideas about improving one's self-esteem that are so prevalent today. Most parents do the best they can for their children with the resources they have. But they make mistakes, are fallible, just as are we.

If you have deep hurts, you may not come to a breakthrough just by putting the past behind you. Get hold of some books about forgiveness and grace. Write down what you feel in your journal. Think about the *good* things your parents passed on to you. You may decide you need further counseling to work through some issues, and that is a good thing to seek. Don't wait, do it as soon as possible.

In any case, no matter how complex, remember that God knows what your burden is. He wants to give you His peace. He is the one who will ultimately remove the weight from your shoulders.

Embraceable You

There's another person you may need to forgive. Look in your mirror.

It's easy enough to acknowledge that we all make mistakes. It's a lot harder to admit that we'll probably make the same mistake over and over. It's easy to say we're all sinners. It's tougher to look hard at ourselves and see the meanness, laziness, anger, a judgmental spirit, pride, whatever may be our downfall.

The problem with false guilt ("I'll never be a good enough mother"), is that it sometimes blinds us to *earned* guilt ("I sometimes say hurtful things to others"). That's the kind of guilt that requires true confession, so we can be cleansed. Our evangelical churches miss something, I think, because they don't normally use the great liturgies of confession, such as "We have left undone those things we ought to have done . . . O Lord, have mercy on us."

A PRAYER OF COMMITMENT

Lord, I'm tired of half-loving, half-complaining about my life. You know I'm just plain tired, Father. I want to live fully for you as your dearly loved child, and I want to start now. Help me to care for myself as you care for me. Help me to make time for myself, to nurture the gifts you've given me, to, above all, seek your peace. Help me to stop being so hard on myself and to start resting in you. I love you, Lord. In Jesus' name I pray. Amen.

On your retreat away, why not take a prayer book or hymnal with liturgy in the back and say some of the words aloud to God. They aren't healing or cleansing in and of themselves, of course, but if spoken from the heart they are. Sometimes we need a framework for our prayers. In any case, know that God forgives you and sent his Son to die for *you*.

If God forgives you, you must forgive yourself. Maybe you haven't achieved all your dreams. You may be wondering what you've really done with your life; perhaps in some respects you've failed. But wait! Look back on what you *have* accomplished. (Write them down.) Some examples: I raised good kids. I've made my husband happy. I've kept some lifelong friends. I've grown in the Lord. You may be simply moving toward some accomplishments. You've made a start. That's something to celebrate too.

We are each a mixed bag of sorts. I, for one, can be deeply compassionate, but I can also be selfish—something I don't like in myself. (Does anybody?) I can be a whirlwind of energy, or on the lazy side; and I don't like *that* in myself, either. But I'm trying, as a recovering "guiltaholic," to recognize my limitations. Of course I'll never be perfectly energetic or wholly compassionate. But I can be less lazy, less selfish, and substitute positive habits for the negative ones.

It's all any of us can do—try, trust, and know that God loves us so deeply that He died for us and is working in us "to will and to do of His good pleasure."

Tomorrow

A few years ago a contemporary Christian album came out with the title, "The Future's So Bright, I Gotta Wear Shades." I laughed when I saw it, but it conveys the attitude Christians can adopt toward the future—not because the world is so great, but because our God is so great!

On that retreat you're going to take—or whenever you have some quiet time—think about tomorrow. *Your* future. What do you see?

I confess I don't always think long-range. Sometimes

the farthest ahead I get is thinking that I should take Amanda for her measles booster before the school year is over in three months! There's so much of the immediate that crowds in on us that we don't have the luxury of pondering the future. Besides, the future can seem so big and unknown, like a medieval map that shows a flat earth surrounded by an ocean marked "Here There Be Dragons."

When I think of the year 2000 looming before me, my turning fifty, dying my gray hair, and Amanda becoming a teenager . . . Our country continuing its moral downhill slide . . . When I think about these things I get depressed, draw my drapes, and go into my warm kitchen and eat a lot of dessert . . . (Anybody else do that?)

You may be one of those rare persons with a detailed, five-year life plan. If it works for you, fine. But if you're like most of us, and you're vague, or even intimidated about what the future holds, I suggest you forget a time-line and concentrate instead on what you'd like to accomplish. Don't worry about the when or the how just yet. Write it down, if that solidifies it for you, and post it on your fridge, or tuck it away in a safe place.

I would like to write more books, including a series for children. It excites me to think about it. I'd like to travel more. I've never seen the Pacific Northwest, Alaska under the midnight sun, Ireland, the Carolinas in spring. I've even thought it would be interesting to have a radio show someday. My husband and I have talked about teaming up in some kind of ministry.

Some plans have more basis in current reality than others, but that's not the point. In fact, Corrie ten Boom once said, "I set out to do as many as sixteen impossible things someday—and I think I did one."

That's not bad!

Your List of Impossible Hopes

What's on your "hope list"? Is any of it impossible? What would move it into the realm of the possible?

Someone has said that the most important things in life are to have "someone to love, something to work for, something to hope for."

Christians don't lack for Someone to love, and Someone who loves us. What are you working for, toward? What are your goals, your dreams? What do you hope for? You need an energizing hope that gets you out of bed in the morning and gets you excited about tomorrow. Maybe we don't need sunglasses as we face the future, but we might have to squint a little!

———

Before I finish here, I want to tell you about another dream I've been having lately: I don't dream about the starving bird anymore. I dream I'm in a house. A house I'm familiar with—not mine, but maybe my grandmother's. It's big and old and rambling. I'm walking down the hall, exploring the rooms, when suddenly I come upon a door I've never seen before. I open it . . . and there's a room I never knew was there! *All these years, and I never discovered this room,* I think. Sometimes it's a beautiful bedchamber, fragrant with perfume. Sometimes it's a large, paneled family room with a stone fireplace and leather furniture. The dream is living-color real to me, and I am happy in it. It's as though I've finally unlocked all the doors in this beloved house.

I believe those rooms are the parts of myself that I'm just beginning to explore. I'm learning to love myself more, fear less, even be a little bold. No one in the dream is telling me "you can't" or "you shouldn't." And no one is clamoring for my attention.

I guess I've come a long way. I hope you're getting there, too.

You don't have to run away from home. You can *come home* . . . to freedom, to healing and wholeness and balance. Open the door to that secret room.

When you do, you may just hear some delighted laughter from the One who wants you to care for yourself as He cares for you.

BOOKS TO LOVE

Here's an entirely arbitrary, subjective list of books and authors to inspire you, absorb you, stretch your imagination and enlarge your vision of God:

Gift From the Sea, by Anne Morrow Lindbergh

A Circle of Quiet, by Madeleine L'Engle

The Seven Storey Mountain, by Thomas Merton

Pilgrim at Tinker Creek, by Annie Dillard

The poetry of Gerard Manley Hopkins

Voyage of the Dawn Treader, by C. S. Lewis; also his space trilogy

Markings, by Dag Hammarskjold

Longing for Love, by Ruth Senter

Anything by Walter Wangerin, Jr., but especially his fiction

The Furniture of Heaven, by Mike Mason

The poetry of Emily Dickinson

Stories for the Christian Year, edited by Eugene Peterson

Old hymnals from different traditions, like the Shakers

And . . .

Children's books:

Anything by E. B. White

Anything by Katherine Paterson

Anne of Green Gables, by L. M. Montgomery

The Moffat books, by Eleanor Estes